first

MATT CARVEL

10 Publishing
a division of 10ofthose.com

First published 2014 by 10Publishing
Copyright © 2014 by Matt Carvel and 10Publishing

ISBN 978-1-909611-79-5

Designed by stevedevanedesign.com

Printed in the UK by CPI Group (UK) Ltd, Croydon, CR0 4YY

10Publishing, a division of 10ofthose.com
9D Centurion Court, Farington, Leyland, PR25 3UQ,
England
Email: info@10ofthose.com
Website: www.10ofthose.com

Contents

1

Your Life and God's Plan

I'm writing this on A-level results day. Around the country there are thousands of young men and women who are celebrating getting into their first choice of university. There are thousands more who are frantically trying to find out whether they got in somewhere even though they haven't got the grades they hoped for. And there are many too who have missed out on their top choice or even their second choice and are going through clearing in order to get on to a course they want to do.

Whatever category you've been in, it's tempting to think that which uni you end up at is all down to you. *But God sees things a little differently.*

There's a proverb in the Bible (Proverbs 19:21) that says although we can make many plans, ultimately it's God's plan that prevails. Your results may have been a surprise to you, but they weren't a surprise to God. He knew which uni you were going to end up in. Not only that, but He's put you there.

Acts 17 explains that God determines the times and places that people live (vv. 26–27). Things like this don't just happen randomly or by accident; God's hand is in all of it.

One of the most encouraging verses in the entire Bible is where God promises that in every situation He is working for our good (Romans 8:28).

Maybe you feel discouraged or deflated because you've ended up somewhere you never really wanted to go. Maybe you're ecstatic because you achieved your first choice. You must understand that either way God has been directing your steps. To Him you're exactly where you need to be right now and He's working for good in your situation.

A VERY ACTIVE GOD

God has got a purpose for you to fulfil. Not only does God determine where we live, but when we look closely at Acts 17 we read that God's reason for placing us where we are is so people might get to know Him for themselves. God has placed you at university for the purpose of His mission.

We make a big mistake if we imagine that God is inactive in the world today. He's not just up there somewhere in the clouds, biding his time, listening to prayers and occasionally answering them. He's committed to His mission and purpose and is actively bringing it about.

What is that mission? It's all about building His church through spreading the Gospel of Jesus Christ.

I'm sure you know this, but it bears repeating. Jesus said, 'I will build my church' (Matthew 16:18). That's what He's promised to do. His last instruction to His disciples was 'go and make disciples of all nations' (Matthew 28:19) and then He sent the Holy Spirit to empower them in this mission. This radical movement that started with the eleven remaining disciples has now spread to millions worldwide.

Every day thousands of people become Christians. The Bible says the Good News of Jesus will keep on spreading until all the nations and people groups have heard it, and then Jesus will return.

God is working towards this end through the

Holy Spirit today. He's got a lot of work to do, but He's committed to it. Yet it won't last forever. One day, when Jesus returns, the time for mission will be over. Until that day, though, there's a lot to be getting on with. The amazing thing is that God has chosen to work through ordinary Christians like me and you.

Maybe you've never thought of yourself as part of an international people movement spanning thousands of years. Maybe you haven't ever looked beyond your own Sunday church experience to realise the world-changing revolution that you're part of. But if you're a Christian, you are part of it.

God's put the Gospel of Jesus Christ in your life and He's put His Holy Spirit in you too. He's given you gifts and talents, energy and faith; and He's put a calling on your life to be a light in a dark place and to live and speak for Him.

ME, A MISSIONARY?

Jesus was the first missionary, sent by God the Father to show the way to salvation and eternal life. At the start of the book of Acts, He hands on that task to His disciples; they are to finish the work He started.

Every disciple, therefore, is a missionary. If you

follow Jesus, that means you too!

Thinking of yourself as a missionary might sound a bit odd, but it's the way God sees you. He's made known to you His Good News and sent you to thousands of people who have no idea how good it is. You've not just ended up at uni; you've been sent there by God for a purpose.

The question is: are you going to follow God's calling and live out this destiny in these next three or so years, or are you going to shy away from it and pretend God hasn't spoken it?

At uni you'll probably meet Christians who are really only that in name. They might have been brought up going to church, but when it comes to actively following Jesus in their daily lives, frankly they've got other priorities.

We mustn't forget that Jesus called His disciples to take up their crosses and follow Him. In some ways there's nothing easier than giving your life to Christ. There is no barrier to God that's not simply overcome by repentance and simple faith in the person of Jesus. But Jesus is quite clear that there's a cost involved in following Him. It won't always be plain sailing; it's going to challenge and stretch you. You'll suffer loss in this life, but ultimately what you'll gain is infinitely more valuable.

Listen to Jesus' words to His followers:

As the Father has sent me, I am sending you. (John 20:21)

These are words with big implications and are tremendously exciting. At uni you might be the only Christian in your halls. You might be the only Christian that your new uni friends will meet. It's often been said that for every person who reads the Bible there's a thousand more who'll read a Christian instead.

God has placed you at uni as His representative. He's going to help you and give you all the strength you need, but He invites you to respond to His call when He says the word, 'go' (Matthew 28:19)!

WHEREVER YOU ARE, BE ALL THERE

It's time to embrace your calling. However you ended up at uni, God extends this call to go and make disciples to you, exactly where you are right now.

The best way you can fulfil that is to be 'all in' at uni. Don't try to be half in, half out. Whatever situation you find yourself in, be all there.

When you come to uni, it can be tempting to try and hold on to the familiar. We might be tentative about finding a new church because we're still holding on to our old one. We might just try and find Christian friends because that feels like the safe option. We might be tempted to go home at weekends and rely on our parents as much as we can.

While there's nothing wrong with loving your old church, Christian friends or your parents, living like this puts you in danger of missing out on the new adventure that God has got for you.

In the book of Jeremiah we learn about how God's people had to leave their home (see 2:37, for example). They thought it was a disaster! I'm sure they were frightened about what a big move would mean. But even though they were going to live in the land of their enemies (which makes your move to uni seem like a walk in the park!) God still had a plan.

When they got to this new country and everything was new and different, you might have expected God to warn His people not to get involved with any of the locals. But He tells them the exact opposite – settle down, build houses, start families and make your future here because this is all part of my plan (Jeremiah 29:4–11).

Be where you are 100 per cent; that was God's advice to His people in exile. Make the most of it in every way you can.

For you at uni, what does that look like? Well,

I'm not suggesting you adopt every practice of uni life (as I explain in later chapters) but I do want to encourage you to get stuck in to university and to get stuck in to following Jesus and being a missionary for Him. Are you ready for an adventure?

Maybe you think God should have picked and sent someone else to your uni instead of you. When you're surrounded by thousands of students, the task can seem a bit daunting! But let's remember that Jesus picked twelve very ordinary, local people to be His first disciples. Just read through the gospels and you'll see plenty of examples of them making mistakes, missing the point and arguing with each other. Almost all of them abandoned or denied knowing Jesus by the time of His death.

I'm sure you're aware of your own faults too, but God wants us to realise that being imperfect makes us perfect candidates to be used by Him. The Bible is full of weak people that God used in incredible ways. All they had to do was follow His call and trust Him.

The Bible says that Jesus is the great reconciler, which means He's in the business of bringing sinful people into a relationship with God. But it goes on to say that He's given us 'the ministry of reconciliation' (2 Corinthians 5:18). We're part of the family business! It's time to learn the tools of the trade.

Treat your halls, flat, lecture or seminar rooms as your new home. It's your unique patch to live out this mission for Jesus. The adventure is about to begin.

2

The Wide and the Narrow Gate

Enter through the narrow gate. For wide is the gate and broad is the road that leads to destruction, and many enter through it. But small is the gate and narrow the road that leads to life, and only a few find it.
(Matthew 7:13–14)

Most of what student life is known for in this country is found through the wide gate and on the broad road, that is the easy way, which Jesus describes in His Sermon on the Mount. There are many who walk along it and few are even looking for the narrow gate.

If you're a Christian and a student, or soon to be one, these two gates and roads are laid out ahead of you and you've got a choice to make. Which will you choose: the wide or narrow gate? The easy road or the hard one?

If you choose the wide and easy way, you'll have a lot of company. Not only are the vast, vast majority of students in Britain unsaved, but devastatingly even the majority of teenage church-goers who arrive at uni see this wide gate of freedom and opportunity opening up to them and join the crowds as they hurry through. According to research in 2011 by the CUE project, 73 per cent of Christian students don't connect to church or any Christian group at university.

Because you've picked up this book, hopefully something in you is urging you to live differently. You might be in the minority, but while the easy way leads to destruction, the hard way – and yeah, it's hard –at least means you walk it with Jesus, right? If you think like that, then this book is for you.

A LIGHT IN THE DARK

Student life can be pretty dark, spiritually speaking. In a lot of ways it's a celebration of sin and the exact opposite of what God wants for young lives that He has made. But the good news is that in dark places a light can shine brightest.

I believe God is calling a generation of young men and women to live a different kind of life and shine brightly for Him – not as moralistic, judgemental crusaders for holy living, but as students who believe in and enjoy the radical goodness of the life that Jesus calls 'life … to the full' (John 10:10). It won't be easy, but it will be worth it.

I believe this because I know that God called me to such a life, and I've seen Him call hundreds, if not thousands, of other eighteen-year-olds in the same way. He's calling you, too. Maybe that's why you picked up this book.

I've spent the last seven years in 'student ministry', as some people call it. Three of those years were as a student myself and four have been working full time for a church. The reason I've done that is because God underlined to me, early on, the unique potential of this stage of life.

For most students the three years between eighteen and twenty-one (or thereabouts) are the time they:

live independently for the first time;

make key decisions about their career, partner and location;

define their principles and values as an adult.

At uni students are setting the trajectory of the next decade of their lives and often beyond that too. Despite the challenges of being a Christian at university, there really is no better time to get to know God and follow Him wholeheartedly.

But how do you do that? As Christians we know that the Bible helps us to live a life that pleases God. In one of the psalms God's Word is described as 'a lamp for my feet' (Psalm 119:105) – God sheds light on the road ahead of us. Great! But the not-so-good news is that often the Bible gives us general wisdom rather than specific instructions. And if we're going to walk the 'narrow road' through the student world, a lot of the time-specific instructions are exactly what we need.

DIRECTIONS FOR THE NARROW ROAD

During my years working with students, I've been asked loads of questions by those who are trying to work out how to walk as a Christian and are wondering how the Bible can help them make good decisions. What I've really wanted is a resource that provides some answers! Unfortunately I haven't found one. So instead I've written one myself and *First* is the result. It sounds quite official, doesn't it? But I just want to give students something that will help them – something that I wish I had when I started uni.

This book is an attempt to bridge this gap I've been talking about – the gap between the Bible's Truth and real university life. Essentially this guide is an answer to the question, 'What does it look like to be a Christian at university?'

My desire is that it helps you to make the most of being at uni, and most of all to spend your time living wholeheartedly for God. Are you ready to take up that challenge?

To some observers being a Christian at university looks like a deliberate exercise in denying yourself pleasure. I'm not going to kid you; following Christ is full of sacrifice, danger, struggle and even disappointment sometimes. But it's also rich in joy, excitement and the unsurpassable experience of God Himself. Are you ready for that kind of life? The last thing it will be is boring.

I pray this guide will help you navigate the road less travelled.

Part One: Wisdom on Key Areas in Uni Life

3

Quality Time with God

Watch and pray so that you will not fall into temptation. The spirit is willing, but the flesh is weak. (Matthew 26:41)

If you're anything like me, the challenge of spending quality time with God each day is the biggest battle in your life. And let's face it, I know you *are* like me because Jesus Himself says our 'flesh is weak'.

Growing up in a Christian family, the importance

of prayer and Bible reading was drilled into me. It's just what Christians do – that was my simple conclusion. Maybe you've recently become a Christian and you've picked up on that too. Often Christians know, in their head, that they *should* read the Bible and pray, but struggle to put that principle into practice.

When you move to university, you're free from boundaries and restraints like never before. What you do with your time is up to you. Eating, sleeping, studying, social time, hobbies – these are all down to your decisions, and most things, you'll discover, are extremely flexible. Cereal for dinner, sleeping in the afternoon, studying at midnight and playing computer games at 4 a.m. were all part of my uni life. I'm sure you have or will have your own unique habits. But in the chaos of this kind of living, spiritual disciplines, as they're sometimes called, can easily be neglected.

Even now as a working man, when life is more structured, I can easily leave them out of my day. Why is it so easy to do that? It's not like reading the Bible or talking to God is a physically demanding or complicated thing to do, is it? But it's the biggest challenge in my life because I know, deep down, that it's the most *important* thing in my life. And the Enemy knows that too, so everything that's sinful in me wants me to keep away from it.

But let's not get caught up with the *doing* before we remember the reason *why*. I'm not a Christian because I've chosen to live a certain way or believe in particular religious principles. At the heart of Christianity is the wonderful truth that God has adopted me – and all other Christians – into His family because of His incredible love. Even though it cost Him His Son, Jesus, God wanted to rescue me so that I'd *be with Him* forever – not so that I could *do* stuff for Him (He doesn't need help with anything!) but so that I could just *be* with Him. Relationship is at the heart of Christianity.

Our purpose in life (and in eternity) is to be with Him, to enjoy Him and to revel in the goodness of knowing the Maker of everything. Your devotional life is where you put everything else aside and take quality time to do just this.

Listen! Prioritise your devotional life. Spend time with God each day. Don't let 'attending Christian meetings' become your Christianity. Invest in *your* relationship with God. I know there are tonnes of things at uni that can distract you, but fight against the temptations. It's so worth it.

The reality is (unless you're studying medicine or something similarly crazy) you actually have loads of free time. You've got an amazing opportunity and a luxury of time you probably won't have again until you retire. Use it while you can.

So, what does spending time with God look like? Well, relating to God is different for every Christian, that's just what relationships are like. You'll have preferences of what time of day and what style suits you best, so I don't want to give too many specific instructions. But here's some advice based on my own experience.

1. PLAN

I'm guessing that before you came to uni you never kept a diary. I don't mean a 'dear diary' diary, I mean a timetable of what you're doing and when. You probably haven't needed to. But at some point you'll realise that to make the best use of your time, to avoid forgetting stuff and to do everything you need to get done, planning your time is essential.

I wouldn't say that I'm naturally organised but I reached a point in my uni life where I had so many things on I just had to plan my week and keep a diary. It's one of those 'life skills' that everyone bangs on about, so you might as well embrace it now and set up a Google calendar or whatever.

Anyway, the point is if you want to prioritise quality time with God, you're going to have to schedule it. Ok, I know that sounds a bit 'unspiritual' to make an 'appointment with God', but it's really not. You arrange to meet your friends, don't you? I make appointments with my wife all the time – we schedule in our 'date night' – but it doesn't make the experience any less meaningful. We schedule it because if we don't, other stuff crops up and we'll lose it.

You can still have spontaneous times with God, but if you just rely on spending time with Him when you feel like it, you probably won't spend much time with Him at all.

So pick a time each day to pray, worship or read the Bible, and enjoy daily appointments with God. It doesn't even have to be the same time each day and it doesn't even have to be every day. Just make it work for you. You won't regret it.

2. DON'T BE OVER-AMBITIOUS

Everyone who competes in the games goes into strict training. They do it to get a crown that will not last; but we do it to get a crown that will last forever. Therefore I do not run like someone running aimlessly; I do not fight like a boxer beating the air.

No, I strike a blow to my body and make it my slave so that after I have preached to others, I myself will not be disqualified for the prize. (1 Corinthians 9:25–27)

The Bible says spiritual disciplines are just like exercise. So, say I was fat and lazy (some people do, actually) but I wanted to run a marathon, where would I begin? I wouldn't set out on a ten-mile run tomorrow, would I? I'd start with a jog round the block and hopefully not keel over before I made it home.

So, if you're out of shape spiritually (i.e. you're not used to spending time with God each day), don't think you can solve your problem with an ambitious action plan. Five chapters into Leviticus you'll keel over and give up.

Little and often is the best way to start. Ten minutes a day can absolutely change your life – I'm serious. If you do ten quality minutes a day with God, even on just five days out of every seven, you'll go from strength to strength in your walk with God.

Five portions of ten minutes a day is far better than an hour once a week, even though it's actually less time. Why? Well, it would take another book to really explain and no-one's got time for that, so just believe me - it is! Try it and you'll find out for yourself – it's life-changing stuff.

You want to do twenty minutes a day? Thirty even? Great, go for it! But just make sure you've got the stamina for it. If in doubt, set small goals, achieve them and then increase them as you go. You'll soon be building muscle in the spiritual gym of life!

3. GET A BALANCED DIET

Some Christians, like me, find reading the Bible not much of a problem, but prayer can be a real slog. For others they'd rather spend half an hour in prayer than five minutes in God's Word. Some find just worshipping God flows naturally and nothing is better than sticking a Christian album on and singing along to Jesus. And some hate singing but thrive in running through a list of prayer requests to God.

Whatever comes easiest to you, it's important to realise that all these ways of relating to God are necessary for an effective and fruitful devotional life. Just scan through the book of Psalms and you'll find all of these elements: praise and worship; meditating on God's Word; asking God for stuff; confessing sin; and just being honest with where you're at and asking Him for help.

Remember that praying, worshipping and reading the Bible is not the end goal. All of these are just methods of connecting with God. And when we connect with God, we get in step with what He's doing in our lives, and we co-operate with the work of the Holy Spirit in making us more like Jesus. And what could be better than that?

Right, I've told you what to do but not how, haven't I? Well, flick to chapters eleven and twelve and you'll find practical tools that will help you to pray and get the most out of reading the Bible. Another good idea is to ask other Christians what they do. I'm sure you'll pick up some great habits from mature Christians that you know.

Real stories from real students

While writing this book, I asked students from my church to tell me about their own experiences. I thought it would be helpful to include some of their responses here. So at the end of several of these chapters you'll find some comments written by real students about their real uni life over the last few years. I hope it sheds some more light on what it's really like and helps you to put the principles I'm talking about into practice.

Perhaps unusually, my first year of uni was really where my devotional life eventually got some rhythm and routine. After sitting through countless talks on the importance of prayer and Bible reading, I knew the stuff inside out but had never managed to make things stick. Uni was the first place I really felt the need to press into God each morning and tangibly felt the difference when I didn't. Because the first term of uni was so new and challenging, I found that my confidence in God and my peace in Him would quickly disappear and so I learnt to value my morning times with Him, however brief.

I heard it said that we will all prioritise and pursue something if we believe that it's worth it, if we can see the value in it, and for me that penny eventually dropped in midst of the challenges of uni.

I found carving out time in my hectic schedule of university life to spend time with God to be so important and crucial for my relationship with God. I found often that my time was so precious, as I was involved in so many different things, so I had to really fight for this time with God to remain a priority. I had to get into a routine that suited me.

I used to love taking my iPod and walking up the hills behind campus. Being surrounded by His creation and looking over campus would really draw me into His presence and motivate me to pray. I kept a journal of all that God was speaking to me about and listed all my prayer requests. It's amazing looking back over those three years to see the journey that I went on spiritually and His hand so clearly with me through that entire season. One thing that really helped me and my devotional life was to be accountable about it with my friends too, often in a small group context. Often we'd go through the same books together to check up on one another and to help spur each other on.

4

Finding a Church

So you arrive at uni, likely with an encouragement to find a local church from Christian parents (if you have them) still ringing in your ears. 'Yeah, I probably should,' you think. But then you've just been thrown together with a bunch of other new students, they're not interested in church and you want to make good friendships, so shouldn't you prioritise them?

It'll only be awkward to find a new church, you reckon, and besides, 'I'm only here for part of the year; I'll just go when I'm back home in the holidays – and make sure I look at my Bible a few times while I'm at uni.'

That may not be every Christian student's experience, but I'm sure it rings true for many. I said earlier that 73 per cent of Christian students fail to get stuck into a church at university. That's crazy! And it shows that finding a church is way down the priority list for most Christian students. So why should you? Here are just three reasons.

1. TO BE A CHRISTIAN IS TO BE PART OF THE CHURCH

… Christ loved the Church and gave himself up for her … (Ephesians 5:25)

And let us consider how we may spur one another on towards love and good deeds, not giving up meeting together, as some are in the habit of doing, but encouraging one another – and all the more as you see the Day approaching. (Hebrews 10:24–25)

Jesus didn't die on the cross so that *individuals*

could become believers; He died for the *church*. Christianity is not an individual pursuit; it's about being part of a God-centred community.

Jesus didn't pass on the gospel message to one random guy; He chose the twelve disciples to be with Him. When He went back to heaven, they carried on gathering, and new converts weren't just 'saved' but were 'added' to the community. You might be saved but are you added to a local community of believers?

2. COMMUNITY IS THE CONTEXT FOR GROWTH AND MATURITY

Rather, in humility value others above yourselves, not looking to your own interests but each of you to the interests of the others.

(Philippians 2:3–4)

'One another' is pretty much a catchphrase in the New Testament. From Jesus' teaching through to the letters there is a constant exhortation to serve, teach, encourage, rebuke, disciple, befriend and pray for one another in the church

Are you sometimes sceptical of how much you'll 'get out of' church? You're thinking about it the wrong way round. God encourages us not to be takers but to be givers. In a local church there are loads of opportunities to serve, encourage others, disciple and be discipled, and ironically it's by *giving* yourself in this way that you actually get the most out of it anyway.

3. TO JOIN A CHURCH IS TO PARTNER IN A MISSION

Jesus is the first missionary, sent by the Father to bring us the Good News. But at the end of Jesus' ministry, He shocks His disciples by saying,

As the Father has sent me, I am sending you. (John 20:21)

Jesus sends the disciples together – it's not a solo mission – and empowers them with the Holy Spirit to be the church. They're not supposed to be an inward-looking believers' club but a society-impacting community with Good News to share. So to not be part of a local church is to miss out on the central purpose of Christianity – to share and celebrate Jesus Christ.

I know there are lots of new things to pursue and spend your time on at uni: friendships, sports teams, societies, studies, etc. But if you're wise, you'll still have plenty of time to be involved with them as well as being fully stuck into church. The local church is just too important to miss out on. Find one today and give yourself to it heart and soul – you won't regret it.

So you make church your priority – got that? But what about campus-based groups like Christian Unions? Should you bother with them?

Sometimes there's confusion or even scepticism when it comes to that kind of question. My advice is very much 'get involved' and here's why.

To begin with, it's important that you understand what CUs are and what they're not. Sometimes people join them purely to make Christian friends (or 'more than friends' – let's be honest). Others even see them as a replacement to being part of a local church. But this is not what they're intended to be. UCCF, who support Christian Unions across the country and do fantastic work, are very clear about what a CU is and isn't. Firstly, they stress that they are not a church, so all CU members should be part of a local church. Secondly, the vision of the CU is to be a mission team at university.

Christian Unions, when they're doing what they're supposed to do, aim to give every student at uni the chance to hear and respond to the

Gospel of Jesus Christ. That's amazing! CUs around the country put time and effort, prayer and money into achieving that goal and I reckon you should give yourself to that as well.

But wait a minute, isn't that also the goal of the local church? Surely the church wants to reach everyone with the Gospel, including students? Why do I need to join a CU to be involved in student mission?

Well, to be honest, you don't *need* to be in a CU to be involved in student mission, but it helps! As well as the training, resources and encouragement that UCCF and CUs provide, the fact is Christian Unions have an access and opportunity on campuses that churches don't. In most cases a church can't work publicly on campus. They can't run evangelistic events, publicly witness or advertise, but as a student society CUs can!

Christian Unions have an open door to share the Gospel in university buildings and so we mustn't miss out on this amazing opportunity. The Gospel is too important. In the Bible we see the great evangelist Paul using 'all possible means' (1 Corinthians 9:22) to reach people with the message of Jesus, so follow his example and get involved with your CU.

If you do join yours but find that it's not focused

on mission and is more of a Christian club, don't give up straight away. Try and be part of the solution. Sign up, go along, make friends and, if no one else is, take the initiative with evangelism. If your CU isn't very mission focused, it probably isn't because they don't want to be but is because no one's bold enough to make the first move. Why not gather anyone who's interested and pray together, beginning by asking God for boldness, wisdom and opportunities to share Jesus with students at your uni? Most students only have three years to be part of a CU so make the most of this unique opportunity and make Jesus known on your campus.

Real stories from real students

One bit of advice I was given was to find a church quickly! This was such valuable advice. It was amazing to get immediately rooted into a church community to nurture me, encourage me and welcome me in as I entered a brand new city. I found myself in a completely new season of life – living on my own, making new choices, starting new friendships – and I found that getting into a church quickly really helped this 'settling-in' process and set the foundation for the rest of my degree.

I found community to be so important in these four years – inside and outside church. I decided to lead by example in this area and I was amazed to see that other people started to catch on, which really helped to make friends quickly. I still see those friends now as my closest friends, and it all started right from the beginning.

....

I ended up choosing a particular church purely because I had more friends there. People really reached out to me and I was so thankful for that. It was an unnatural choice for me because I come from a different church background, but as I got stuck in, I realised I agreed with the teaching and theology more than other places I had been.

....

I was really grateful to get quickly stuck into a quality church. I would advise anyone not to spend the first term/year 'church-searching' but to be looking to commit somewhere. Look for a church where you can see God moving and where the people are faithful and excited about His work. No church will be perfect, so know what is important to you then choose to give yourself and get behind the leaders.

5

Study

> The LORD God took the man and put him in the Garden of Eden to work it and take care of it. (Genesis 2:15)

Five chapters in and I *finally* get on to what university is supposed to be all about: learning! Does the Bible have anything to say about your studies? Yeah, it does actually.

It may surprise you to know this (especially if you're reading this in procrastination *from* some work you're meant to be doing) but God made you to work. Work has been His intention for humankind since the beginning.

When we think of the Garden of Eden, we might think of a paradise where Adam and Eve had their feet up and were 'just chillin' with God. But that's not what the Bible actually describes. Genesis 2 says God placed Adam in the garden to work it, and Eve's job was to help him do that (vv. 15,18).

If we read the book of Proverbs, one of the recurring characters is the 'sluggard' – basically a lazy guy who doesn't want to work. He's not exactly praised for his attitude, is he? No. God has given humankind a mandate to work. Likewise you're not a kid anymore – you're at least eighteen – and God wants to put you to work too. At uni, work means studying for your degree.

STUDYING FOR JESUS

There are loads of encouragements in the Bible to apply ourselves to work as if Jesus is our boss and we're working for Him alone (Colossians 3:23). That's a great way to approach it. Why? Because if we're working for Jesus, we naturally want to do our best, but at the same time we know He's sympathetic to our struggles. He forgives us when we don't get it quite right.

One amazing thing about studying for Jesus is that we don't have to worry like other students do. Studies and exams and grades are important – of course they are – and you should do your best. But as a Christian you know that it's not all or nothing.

When you know God is in charge of your life and that in *every* circumstance He is working for our good (Romans 8:28), failing an exam or even a whole year isn't the end of the world. Jesus specifically tells us not to worry because God will provide; He just wants us to trust Him:

So do not worry, saying, 'What shall we eat?' or 'What shall we drink?' or 'What shall we wear?' For the pagans run after all these things, and your heavenly Father knows that you need them. But seek first his kingdom and his righteousness, and all these things will be given to you as well. Therefore do not worry about tomorrow, for tomorrow will worry about itself. Each day has enough trouble of its own. (Matthew 6:31–34)

SUCCESS REDEFINED

So work hard, don't be lazy, be diligent in your studies, apply yourself (whatever that means), do the best you can and make the most out of your degree, but don't make grades your standard of 'success' in uni life. For the Christian success is growing closer to God and faithfully trusting Him with every aspect of our lives. Sure, pray for God's help when you're struggling, but also pray that He'd help you not to worry and to trust your life to Him whatever happens.

For me, I finished my degree and got a 2:1. I was happy with that. I was pleased because I had worked hard and got a good grade. But if I'm honest, I reckon I could have got a first. So why am I happy with less than that?

Well, to get a first I would have had to pretty much spend most waking hours of my second and third year in intense study. But I knew that as well as my degree God had brought me to uni to be a witness for Him. So actually I devoted a lot of time to the Christian Union, church small groups, Bible study and evangelism. I also had hobbies like playing in a band. I don't regret any of that. Maybe sometimes I didn't get the balance totally right, but overall I don't think I dishonoured God with the way I used my time.

This balance is a hard one to figure out. It looks different for different students. All I'll say is don't neglect your studies but don't let them define you either. Use them as an opportunity to worship God, ask Him for His help and trust that He will give you grace to live a life that honours Him.

6

Relationships and Singleness

Everyone's built for relationships. That's the way God made us. We all go about it in different ways and maybe some people are more motivated in this area than others, but when it comes down to it we all like to be liked, we all value great friendships and it's always good to have someone to talk to.

When you throw several thousand eighteen- to twenty-one-year-olds together and mix in equal doses of social freedom and alcoholic beverages, the result is thousands of relationships. Many are casual, many are romantic, many are sexual, some are long-lasting and some are quite frankly weird, but whoever you are you'll probably spend far too much of your uni years thinking about them and agonising over them.

I'm going to focus here on boyfriend–girlfriend relationships because, let's face it, you don't need my advice about how to make friends. I'm really not the expert there. If you like football, we're friends in five seconds. If you don't, I'm afraid I'm not quite sure what to say to you.

Actually, I'm not really an expert when it comes to romantic relationships either. Somehow I ended up getting married, which is particularly surprising since Catherine doesn't like football at all. But that's not the point. The point is that, as a student worker, I've found that Christian students ask more questions about romantic relationships than anything else. So here goes: this is my collected wisdom on all that relationship stuff.

WHAT IS 'BIBLICAL DATING'?

You probably don't need me to point out that the general dating/sex/relationship world at uni is pretty far removed from the Bible's point of view. Sex and relationships are generally thought of as just things to make you happy. They're fun, they're for pleasure and, yeah, maybe you can go for something long term if that floats your boat – but hey, no pressure, just 'see what happens'.

How should Christian students react to this? This is a classic example of the wide and narrow road. Which do you want to walk down? There's plenty of room on the wide road, and you'll have plenty of company too, but it will lead to your ruin. If your heart's set on that, there's not much I can say here to dissuade you, so I'm not going to try.

But hopefully you've seen enough of Jesus to want to walk down the narrow road of following Him, even in this pressured area of relationships. OK, let's take a few steps forward. Firstly, are boyfriend–girlfriend relationships even right? When you think about it, the Bible never talks about them, does it? So where do we even start?

The chances are you're probably more informed about 'dating' by American sitcoms than you are by the Bible. The pattern you're most familiar with is the 'hook up/break up/see what feels right/ don't think long term/is he or she right for me?' mentality.

It's so easy to just do relationships the way other people do them and then stick on a little bit of Christianity, like 'we're not going to sleep together'. Now, I'm not knocking drawing some good boundary lines – they're extremely helpful. But even though in the Bible the word 'dating' doesn't appear, the Bible does have a lot to say about romantic relationships, sex and marriage, and it starts with a completely different perspective all together.

The concept of a male–female, romantic, love-filled, sexual relationship belongs to God. We didn't invent shacking up, God did. So if we follow Him, we really should do it like He told us to. Just like with washing your jeans, ignoring the Maker's instructions can lead to a damaging outcome.

The book of Genesis explains that God made men and women and designed them to have an intimate relationship with each other:

That is why a man leaves his father and mother and is united to his wife, and they become one flesh. (Genesis 2:24)

In the very beginning of humankind God made a principle that a man marries a woman; they have children; those children leave their father and mother and find a husband or a wife for themselves; and the process continues. God designs and implements this before sin enters the world. He says, 'Be fruitful and increase in number; fill the earth' (Genesis 1:28) and He says that all his creation is 'very good' (Genesis 1:31).

So according to the Maker, sex and romance are good gifts from God, but are given to men and women in the context of marriage. To take aspects of marriage, like sex, co-dependence and intimacy, and drag them into a non-marital relationship is therefore a distortion of God's gifts and a sin against Him. These aspects, particularly sex and intimacy, are key elements of what we see in present-day 'dating' but, according to God, their proper place is in marriage.

What should Christian dating be like then? Well, if God designs marriage and doesn't settle for anything less in terms of romantic relationships, then it means that the only God-honouring way to 'date' is two people beginning a process of getting to know each other with the aim of marriage.

Friendship is right at the centre of Christian dating and this can be pursued without bringing in aspects that God has ordained to be kept in marriage. Of course, for a boyfriend and girlfriend it is a different type of friendship: it is romantic, it is intentional and it is unique to each of them. But it doesn't pretend to be marriage, nor is it a 'rehearsal' for it. We don't 'try each other on'; we get to know each other, learn to serve each other and take steps to build a friendship that may last a lifetime.

THE BREAK UP

Last a lifetime?! That sounds a bit scary. When I've just started to get to know someone, how can I know whether it's going to work out or not?

It's this type of question that can lead to a great deal of worry in Christian relationships. You probably know the story: there's someone you like, you get to know them a little bit, you realise you fancy them, but what should you do? Are they 'the one'? Will it be really awkward if it doesn't work out? What will everybody who knows us think?

But slow down! Let's think about this. A wrong decision isn't one that doesn't work out the way you thought it would. A wrong decision, biblically, is where we're disobedient to God's will – in other words, where we sin. When it comes to making decisions about who to go out with (or what career to have, or where to live, etc.), it's actually very unlikely that it would be 'wrong' biblically – and if it is wrong, that's usually obvious.

One of the beautiful things about Christian

dating (or whatever you want to call it) is that you can pursue friendship without doing anything that dishonours Jesus or compromises your own purity. For that reason, if you come to a point in a relationship where you realise it's not going to work, you don't have any regrets and it's not been a 'mistake'.

The Bible says, 'Those who honour me, I will honour' (1 Samuel 2:30), so the object of our lives should not be avoiding risky decisions but, in whatever we do, living in a God-honouring way. The thing is you never know the end at the beginning. As 'led' or unsure as you feel at the beginning, it's impossible to be certain if a relationship is going to result in marriage. 'Marriage is success and anything less is failure' is not the way we should think. Failure would be to dishonour Jesus (Colossians 3:17), and sadly many couples do that in the process of dating but end up in marriage anyway.

When I hear about couples who have broken up, of course I feel sad for them. But when I know that they have conducted their relationship in purity, I'm also really encouraged. Maybe in the future they'll each marry someone else; maybe they won't. But at least they've honoured Jesus along the way. In our churches we should prize

God-honouring dating and God-honouring marriage; both are always a 'success' because Jesus gets the glory.

Right, enough about relationships, you're probably not in one right now anyway, are you? (If you are, you might want to flick to chapter ten on 'The Top Five Questions about Relationships'.) Let's talk about singleness instead.

SINGLENESS

Often students rush into relationships too quickly. Especially in Christian circles it can feel like there's a lot of pressure to go out with someone. A few months in to term when people are hooking up all around you, the pressure can almost get too much! You can get the idea that something is wrong with you if you don't have a boyfriend or girlfriend.

But if the Christian's idea of marriage is a friendship that's aimed at marriage, we should definitely not rush into stuff. If you're single, enjoy being single! Don't spend your time envying others and their relationships; be focused on living for God whatever circumstance you're in.

Sometimes there can be an unsaid idea in churches that to be married is better than being single. Therefore a lot of students can put pressure on themselves to be in a relationship with someone they could marry by the time they graduate. Now let's be honest, I've been to a lot of weddings in the last five years, including my own, so it's true that lots of people do meet their future spouse at uni. But please don't get too hung up about it. Being single is actually a great place to be. God thinks so anyway!

Let's have a look at what the Bible has to say about singleness. For a start, the man who wrote more books in the Bible than anyone else was single: the apostle Paul. Jesus Christ was single. How about that for an endorsement? John the Baptist, Jesus' nomination for 'the greatest man that ever lived' (see Luke 7:28), was also single. If you, even for a second, think that being single for part, or the entirety, of your life is in some ways an inferior calling to marriage, then you are gravely mistaken.

Paul, a single man who arguably achieved more for the Kingdom of God than anyone else (aside from Jesus), has these wise words to share with us:

I would like you to be free from concern. An unmarried man is concerned about the Lord's affairs – how he can please the Lord. But a

married man is concerned about the affairs of this world – how he can please his wife – and his interests are divided. An unmarried woman or virgin is concerned about the Lord's affairs: her aim is to be devoted to the Lord in both body and spirit. But a married woman is concerned about the affairs of this world – how she can please her husband. I am saying this for your own good, not to restrict you, but that you may live in a right way in undivided devotion to the Lord.
(1 Corinthians 7:32–35)

Being single is not a second best; it is a unique, God-given opportunity to serve God with undivided attention. I don't think Paul could be clearer here about the drawbacks of being married. When we consider his own life, his missionary journeys, his persecution and imprisonments, it would not have been possible to serve God the way he did had he been married.

If you are single, are you concerning yourself

with the purposes of God? Are you using your freedom to give 'undivided devotion to the Lord'? Let these words challenge and inspire you to action for Him.

Recently I read some advice that I think is pretty good: 'Run as fast as you can towards Jesus, and from time to time look to the side. If you see someone who you fancy *and* who is running the same speed as you, ask them out for a drink.'

So don't slow down for anyone. Some of you will run solo all your life and others will run with someone else along the way. But the most important thing is that you're running for Jesus.

Real stories from real students

....

> For me I suddenly found myself aware of so many more students my age – particularly in church. It was so encouraging but also meant that relationships were bound to happen. During this time it was so important for me to remember to be a witness here to all my housemates and other mates, etc. Housemates were a biggy here as they would see every aspect of my relationship – the physical, the lead-up to the relationship and the on-going

way I handled everything. I found it really helpful to be accountable to some close friends as I walked through this stage and I also made sure I had older and wiser people influencing my life, challenging me and who I was able to be honest with. I personally hate cheesy Christian coffee dates and avoided them at all costs! In my experience the best relationships are those that start out as friends – be natural! I made sure I hung out in groups and really got to know that person in a group setting before I dived deeper and got to know them one to one.

....

I learnt a lot in my second year through a relationship that didn't work out and, even though it was painful, I'm really thankful for the valuable insights and things I learnt about myself through it. Especially if you're moving from a smaller church to a bigger, city-based one, just be sure to keep level headed and be purposeful in relationships you get involved in or dates you go on. Whilst it's totally fine to test the waters, just check whether you genuinely like someone and can see things going somewhere before getting involved. Don't be afraid to turn people down! I've had to learn to trust my heart on these things. I'm now in a long-distance relationship with an amazing guy and I'm so glad for the scary decisions not to settle for anyone else earlier on.

Sex

In the previous chapter on relationships I summed up dating as two people pursuing a friendship with the aim of getting married. This is an exclusive friendship and it is romantic and it is intentional, but it's not 'pretending to be married', so shouldn't include key aspects of marriage like sex, co-dependence and deep intimacy.

The problem is we don't really like this sort of teaching. In some ways *I* don't even like it and here I am telling it to you. No sex in dating? It doesn't completely make sense to us. At worst it feels like 'rules for the sake of rules'. When faced with the question, 'Why can't I have sex with my girlfriend/boyfriend?' the reasoning is often, 'It doesn't hurt anyone, so what's the big deal?'

Well, I could make this book five times longer and try to convince you that this Bible teaching makes sense (and there are some good reasons out there), but really it doesn't, not to a lot of us anyway. Like in a lot of cases, God tells us stuff and we don't really understand His reasons behind it. Just read the Old Testament for five minutes and you'll find loads of examples of where God tells His people to do something but the exact reasons why are unclear. A lot of the time we can't really see the significance of things that seem important to God.

Why does Jesus want us to take communion? Why does He want us to get baptised? God doesn't leave us in the dark about these things, but when you have to explain it to someone who isn't a Christian, it really just boils down to 'because He's told us to'.

As you might expect, I've met a lot more Christians who take issue with God saying that sex should be confined to marriage than have issues with communion. Sadly, because many Christians don't think it *is* a big deal, they disobey what God says about sex. It's not that God doesn't tell us so (the Bible's teaching on sex is as clear as day) but that we think, 'This doesn't make any sense.

Why would God want to deprive me of something good?' So we go ahead and disobey Him. All we need is the voice of temptation to whisper, 'Did God *really* say …' (Genesis 3:1, my italics), and before we know it the opportunity presents itself and we fall into sin.

The question is, like so often in this book, 'Are you going to take God at His word?' Are you going to walk the narrow road of discipline and self-control?

GRACE FOR YOU

I want to encourage you, as much as I can, to follow God and to be obedient to Him in this world of sex and relationships. It flies directly in the face of university culture as much as anything else. It's not easy, but God will help you through. God promises that we won't be tempted more than we can bear (1 Corinthians 10:13). There's always a way out of compromising situations and the Bible's instruction is not just to sidestep sexual temptation but to run in the opposite direction (1 Corinthians 6:18).

But what if you have sinned in this area? What if these words are grating on you because you know you've disobeyed God? How does God respond to you?

Sexual sin can cut deeper than anything else in life. Sometimes it fills us with so much guilt and shame. And sometimes in church life it can feel like it's so shameful that we can't tell anyone about it, so we keep it hidden.

The Good News of the Gospel is that Jesus died for sinners. Every one of us has failed God. None of us have lived up to His teaching and instructions. Listen to me: your sin is not beyond Jesus' forgiveness. It's really not.

For some reason it can be easier to accept God's forgiveness when we first become a Christian. We're aware then for the first time that we need Jesus' love and forgiveness, and so we repent and turn to Him. But once we *are* a Christian, some foolish idea can capture us – we may think that, because we should know better now, when we sin it's somehow worse, and that God won't forgive us, or that He's particularly disappointed with us.

As Christians we can be even more miserable about our sin than when we were unsaved, because we feel a greater sense of letting God down. This leads us to try and put a brave face on our Christianity and to not even tell others that we sin, especially with sexual sin, because the church is the 'holy club'.

I say this because I know what that is like. But the Bible smashes this stupid idea in the first letter of John:

If we claim to be without sin, we deceive ourselves ... (1 John 1:8)

That means you, Christian! If you're pretending that you're sin-free, then you're fooling no one but yourself. God certainly knows that. Stop imagining that you can be perfect this side of heaven – you're not and you won't be. Your sin is not a surprise to God.

But John's instructions don't stop there. Listen to how he continues:

If we confess our sins, he is faithful and just and will forgive us our sins and purify us from all unrighteousness. (1 John 1:9)

Notice that phrase 'all unrighteousness'. Whatever manner of sin you have committed, or even had committed against you, Jesus cleans us from it. 'Yeah, but you don't know how bad it is!' you may argue. My question to you is: is it unrighteous? Yes. So it comes under the category of 'all unrighteousness' and Jesus has promised to wipe it all away.

The only reason Jesus can take our sin away is because He paid its debt on the cross. He died for your sin. And remember the cross stretches both ways: it deals with all your sin of the past and all your sin of the future too.

On the day you got saved, God knew all the sin that you would go on to commit until the day you died. But He still loved you, and He still sent His Son to pay the punishment in advance. He's dealt with it. Jesus' dying words were, 'It is finished' (John 19:30).

If you've committed sexual sin, Jesus can forgive you. My encouragement is to not keep it hidden. Obey John's words and confess it. Confess it to God but it's also helpful to confess it to a trusted Christian friend or pastor. Give it to Jesus, thank Him that He died for it and then stand on the truth that He has cleansed you from all unrighteousness. This is simply another way of taking God at His Word – believing His promises. If He says you're forgiven, don't worry if you don't 'feel forgiven'. If you've repented, believe in Jesus' promise and enjoy the freedom of forgiveness.

PORNOGRAPHY AND MASTURBATION

Before we move on from this subject of sex, I must mention porn. Porn is widespread at uni. It's not a taboo subject these days – it's assumed that you'll watch it.

How should the Christian respond? It almost goes without saying that porn comes under the category of what the Bible calls 'sexual immorality', and therefore the instruction for the Christian is, again, to flee from it.

Some might object and say, 'It's not hurting anyone', but of course it does. It distorts our view of what sex is. It rips it out of the context of commitment, respect and exclusivity in which God has placed it in marriage. And so for single Christians to pursue porn now will be damaging not only to themselves but also to their marriage in the future (if they get married). Like all sin, there is an alluring pleasure. But like bait on a hook, there is also a bite that hurts and traps us.

Addiction to pornography and masturbation (a normally associated activity) cripples Christians, robs them of their joy and quite frankly renders them ineffective for the work of God because they're often so ashamed and caught up in their sin.

Let me also briefly talk about masturbation

directly. Is it a sin to masturbate? Well, the Bible doesn't identify it as such specifically. However, Jesus does have a lot to say about lust (Matthew 5:28) and I don't think you can separate the two things.

God has designed sex as an expression of exclusive love between a husband and a wife. To essentially have sex on your own (or with the help of images on a screen) is therefore a sinful distortion of this.

With this in mind, let me urge you again to pursue forgiveness and freedom through the Gospel. This sexual immorality is no more or less sinful than any other sin, and can equally be dealt with by Jesus. Repeat the above steps of confession, repentance and belief in God's promises, and don't compromise or think you are beyond repair. Please also read chapter twelve: 'Help to Live Porn-Free'.

The Gospel is tailor-made for sinners; that means it's absolutely perfect for people like you and me.

8

Drinking and Drugs

Let me talk next about alcohol for a bit, and as I do bear in mind that these principles apply to other drugs as well. As you'll see, the issue isn't the drug itself but drunkenness (or getting stoned/high/whatever).

DOES GOD CARE ABOUT HOW MUCH I DRINK?

If you ask people to think of uni life in the UK, a lot of them will think of drunk students. We've got a drinking culture. Most social events are built around it and drinking to excess is not just accepted but expected.

As a Christian student, how are you supposed to deal with that? Do you go along with it as much as you can to fit in? It's good to make friends, right? Or should you condemn others' immoral lifestyle, take the high ground and not set foot in a pub or let a drop of alcohol touch your lips?

Sadly a lot of Christian students don't think alcohol is much of an issue. It's certainly not uncommon for students to lift their hands in worship on Sunday but be off their face come 11 p.m. on a Thursday night. Is this a problem? Does God care about drunkenness? Evidently a lot seem to think He doesn't. The familiar argument is: 'God loves me, doesn't He? Being saved is about what He's done, not what I've done or do, yeah? So I get drunk every now and again – what's the problem?'

Though there are elements of truth in this kind of response, it's far from the whole picture. Yes, God *does* love us. But He loves us so much He doesn't want to leave us like we used to be. He doesn't want us to live like everyone else does; He calls us to something better.

For a start, the Bible is quite clear that getting drunk is sin. 1 Peter 4:3 and Galatians 5:21 name drunkenness alongside sex orgies as behaviour that's totally at odds with a Christian life. Galatians 5 also specifically warns us not to abuse the grace and freedom that we have in Jesus by indulging in sinful practices and thinking that it doesn't matter to God. We can't use the idea 'but God loves me anyway' as an excuse to sin.

Paul also talks about this issue in Romans 6:1–2, first asking a question and then answering it:

Shall we go on sinning, so that grace may increase? By no means! We are those who have died to sin; how can we live in it any longer?

How can we as Christians who rely totally upon the grace of God for salvation then go on to abuse the very grace that saves us?

You might think getting drunk isn't a big deal, but it is a big deal to God. Of course, because of His great mercy towards us, He doesn't count our sins against us and all our actions are forgivable. However, in one sense all sin separates us from God. If the Holy Spirit is helping us to walk in one direction, sin is like turning and running the opposite way.

When you get drunk, what you're effectively saying is, 'I'm the most important person in my life.' You're saying that your pleasure is more important than living in a way that honours Jesus. Do you really want to live like that?

HOW SHOULD I RESPOND TO THE BIBLE'S TEACHING?

If you've abused alcohol in the way I've described, you may now be convicted about it. If so, say sorry to God and know that, because of Jesus, He has forgiven you. Amazing!

Sometimes when we repent, we accidentally make the focus of our repentance about us. How? Well, as well as saying sorry, we say, 'I'm never going to do that again!' We make promises to God in an attempt to make up for the way that we feel we've failed Him.

You don't need to do this; in fact, you shouldn't. Because your Christian life is not about your efforts at avoiding sin; it's about being dependent on God. In your own strength you'll probably not be able to keep that promise anyway. Simply ask for God's help to walk closely with Him and not fall into temptation again. Confess not just your sin but your desperate need for Him.

In my life I messed up with alcohol in a big

way. Drinking was a major way of fitting in with friends, being cool, trying to be self-confident, etc. Ultimately it was a symptom of a bigger rebellion against God in my heart.

Incredibly God eventually humbled me enough so I realised the error of my ways and I came back to Him. I then had to face the question of how to live among my friends and not fall into the same temptations as before. I actually decided to give up alcohol completely for a certain amount of months to help me resist the temptation of drunkenness. I'm not saying this is what everyone should do – not at all. I know it just helped me at that time.

But I suppose it does lead me on to the bigger question of whether Christians should drink at all. This is often asked by students, so here are some of my thoughts on it.

SHOULD CHRISTIANS DRINK AT ALL?

Right through the Old and New Testament the 'drunkard' is someone at odds with the wisdom of God and the grace of the Gospel (as can be found from Proverbs 23:20–21 to Titus 1:7). So should we conclude that alcohol is at odds with a Christian's life?

Well, no. It's unlikely that Jesus would have

disapproved of alcohol completely and supplied it so abundantly at the wedding at Cana (John 2) if this were the case. Nor would Paul have advocated being teetotal while advising his protégé Timothy to 'use [drink] a little wine' (1 Timothy 5:23). All good things were made by God. Alcohol is not evil; it was created by God as a blessing to us (1 Timothy 4:4).

At the same time we must acknowledge verses like Romans 14:21:

It is better not to eat meat or drink wine or to do anything else that will cause your brother or sister to fall.

What point is Paul making here? I think he's making two points. Firstly, like everything he writes about, he's saying that the Gospel is the most important thing (1 Corinthians 15:3–4). Secondly, because of this, he's urging us that our behaviour should match it:

Whatever happens conduct yourselves in a manner worthy of the gospel of Christ. (Philippians 1:27)

Therefore, if my drinking causes a friend to fall into temptation and sin, then I am contributing to him bringing the Gospel of Christ into disrepute. The way we live demonstrates the Gospel, so saying we believe it but living in a contradictory way isn't right. It dulls the light that God wants to shine through us (Matthew 5:16).

So let us be wise about our drinking. If it takes anything away from (1) Christ's honour, or (2) the needs of others, then it's better not to drink. There may be times and places that this principle applies.

OK, then *how much* can I drink?

Let me finish by focussing in on a challenging verse that Paul goes on to write in chapter 14 of Romans, verse 23:

… everything that does not come from faith is sin.

Read that again. I told you it was challenging! I mention this verse because an inevitable question that follows from a discussion like this is, 'Well, *how much* can I drink? Where's the line between enjoying a drink and not getting drunk?' I think this is important to ask and I have asked it many times myself!

I think this verse helps us a lot. You see, it tells us that sin is when we take the blessings of God and use them for self-worship rather than in worship of Him.

I know I can have a beer and say, 'Praise God, He is good. He has blessed me with great-tasting beer.' I can maybe even have a second and enjoy it 'with thanksgiving'. When my heart is directed towards God, this is an act that does 'come from faith'. But when it comes to that third or fourth beer, I know in my heart that worshipping God is no longer my desire. My desire is self-promotion. I wish to forget about how God wants me to live my life. My focus is my own ego and how I can feel good despite the consequences. Then there is no faith in my heart and I have fallen in to sin.

I thank God that He is kind and merciful and not only forgives us our sin (1 John 1:9) but has also put the Holy Spirit in us to help us pursue holiness and avoid the selfish desires of the flesh (Romans 7:24–25; 8:1,13–14). Why don't you ask God for His help in this area too?

9

Housing

For most students uni is the first time living away from the family home. Often universities have halls for first-year students, so you don't really get a choice who you end up with. But since most students will rent a house with other students in their second and third year, who to live with soon becomes a big question.

My advice to Christian students is to preferably live with Christians, and definitely to live in a same-sex house: guys with guys, and girls with girls. Let me explain why. I'll start with the single-sex issue because I think it's the most important.

SHOULD I LIVE WITH THE OPPOSITE SEX?

The first reason I advise against guys living with girls is because it can get really awkward. Mixed houses of friends can seem a great idea at first, and when everyone signs the tenancy agreement there's no hint of romantic relationships blossoming. But give it a few weeks and you can almost guarantee someone starts fancying someone else in the house. Then what do you do?

As Christians it's extremely unwise to go out with someone who you live with, so you're kind of stuck. Or maybe the fancying is just in one direction? One housemate asks another out and they say 'no'. Well, that's awkward. And you and your housemates will probably have months left on your tenancy and it won't be much fun because there's embarrassment and broken hearts all over the place.

Now OK, I'm imagining a situation that may not happen. Maybe with you it probably won't. But is it really worth running the risk?

Secondly, and more importantly, I advise against mixed-sex houses on the general principle of not putting yourself in the way of temptation unnecessarily. Housemates coming out of the bathroom in a towel or wandering around in pyjamas, late nights on the sofa and guy–girl friendships can all get a bit blurry in hectic uni life. Maybe you're much holier than me, but it doesn't help me to pursue purity and godliness in thought and deed when I know there's a member of the opposite sex in the shower on the other side of the door. Enough said on that.

Thirdly, there can be lots of great benefits to living in a same-sex Christian house. Proverbs 27:17 says:

> As iron sharpens iron, so one person sharpens another.

Jesus talked often about living alongside one another, being honest with each other, forgiving each other and keeping accountable to one another (see Matthew 18:15–16, 20 and Luke 17:3, for example). In the context of Christian community Ephesians 4:15 encourages us that:

> Instead, speaking the truth in love, we will grow to become in every respect the mature body of him who is the head, that is, Christ.

There is a level of accountability, sharpening, encouraging, discipleship and spurring each other on (see James 5:16, 1 Thessalonians 5:11 and Hebrews 10:24, for example) that can be achieved between brothers or between sisters in Christ that can't be achieved in the same way across genders. I'd encourage you to make the most of this when you have the opportunity.

WHAT ABOUT LIVING WITH NON-CHRISTIANS?

On the subject of 'Christian' houses let me first say we're now verging into my own personal preference here rather than what I think is biblically wise, so please read this for what it is. I've known guys who have made a great job of living with other guys who aren't Christians and they would champion that strongly. But they're not writing this book so you're stuck with my opinion. Here are three reasons I'd recommend living with Christians while at uni.

Firstly, the type of discipleship culture that I've already mentioned is difficult to achieve if there's even just one non-Christian in the house. Just on a practical level you find that often it would be insensitive to non-Christian housemates to pray together, worship or hold small group meetings in your house.

Also, if you are able to have close accountability between the Christians, it can create a divide along faith lines in your house. The Christians are always doing stuff together that the non-Christians aren't. This has the danger of making the non-Christians feel alienated from Christianity, or on the other hand tempts the Christians to tone down their Christian commitment so as not to offend anyone.

Secondly, some argue that living with non-Christians provides a great opportunity to witness to them and share the Gospel. This can be true, and I know of students who have become Christians because of this type of wisdom! However, it doesn't *always* work like this. Don't think that living with someone always makes it easier to talk to them about Jesus. In my experience I've actually found it quite difficult because of the potential to cause disagreement in the house. It can be tempting to not want to 'rock the boat' in a house when you know you've got eleven months left on your tenancy!

Being a red-hot evangelist in your mate's bedroom might be a little too intrusive. While on the other hand talking about Jesus with your friends down the pub can be a little easier when you know that you can shake hands and go to different homes at the end of the evening. On-going dialogue can sometimes be easier when you can give each other space to think and you're not imposing on each other's lives.

Thirdly, while some Christians go and live with a group of non-Christian friends with 'missionary' intentions, sometimes the opposite can happen. The Christian can be more influenced by them than they are for Christ. It's almost impossible not to be influenced by those around us, so it's important that we make sure those influences are positive ones whenever possible.

Having been involved in student work for a number of years, I've known of many guys and girls who have flourished in their faith because they had others around them to keep them accountable and encouraged them to live for Christ. I think this is what Jesus wants for us.

Sadly I've also watched from a distance as many well-meaning Christians have surrounded themselves with bad influences and have stumbled in their faith or even fell away all together.

Now there are exceptions on both sides, but please think carefully about this question of who to live with. Often those who we live with influence us the most, so where are you most likely to grow in your relationship with Jesus?

Real stories from real students

....

I would never have gone to the prayer meetings as much if I didn't live with other Christian guys. I know that's not the best reason to go to the prayer meeting, just because my mates were going, but it really helped motivate me. It wasn't like we really talked about 'accountability stuff' very much, but was just the fact that we were all together, all committed to the church, all involved. It just made it easier for me. Before then I found it really easy to drift in my commitment to God and to church. Just being around guys that shared the importance of that helped me a lot.

....

My second and third years were spent in the same house with (pretty much) the same group of amazing girls. I have been incredibly blessed to have a peaceful and happy house where, even though the group was slightly thrown together, there has been genuine friendship and love. Living with *three non-Christian girls has been brilliant and a great opportunity to share my life and, occasionally, my faith as well as an easy way for them to meet others from my church and hear their stories. I know my situation has been unusually easy, but I wholeheartedly recommend students to take the opportunity to live alongside friends who don't yet know Jesus. Uni is a unique chance to open your lives up to others and I'd say it's been the best part of my uni years. I also live with an incredible and like-minded Christian from my church, which has meant we've been able to support each other and partner up in loving the other girls and coaxing them into church!*

My first day in my first year I arrived at my uni home very nervous and hoping to share something in common with my four other housemates. I entered the house to find (forgive the crass stereotyping) a Nigerian, a Moroccan 'rudeboy', a 'militant atheist' goth and a thirty-five-year-old homosexual. The year that followed was a peculiar one, although somehow I got along really well with all of them and became the peacemaker for all the in-house drama. It only brought me closer to the heart of God for all varieties of people.

....

I think it's really important to live with people you firstly get along with! Some friends of mine had 'made pacts' with people from day one about living arrangements. I didn't want to limit myself to one particular group of friends – especially as I found that these friendships changed so much during the first term. I found it was helpful to wait until at least after Christmas before thinking about who to live with.

I made sure I had a balance of Christian and non-Christian housemates in my house. I wanted to be intentionally available to be a witness to those that weren't yet Christ followers. Just by living with me they picked up so much of my life and had a front seat in seeing how Jesus was such an important part of my life. But I'm so grateful that I had a spiritual sister with me too. We were able to encourage each other, look out for one another and just be a 'team in this process', which is so helpful as often it can become *quite a vulnerable environment to be in. We made sure we not only prayed for our housemates but also made a point of praying in the house, which makes such a difference!*

....

I lived in university halls my first year and then with non-Christians in my second year. Although it was tough at times I am glad I did it. I found that the way I reacted to life events, stresses and problems really helped my friends to see who I really was and how much of a help having God is in my life.

Part Two:
Practical Tools
for Uni Living

10

The Top Five Questions about Relationships

1. WHAT SHOULD I LOOK FOR IN A BOYFRIEND/GIRLFRIEND?

There's a concept of 'compatibility' that has become so exaggerated by our culture that it is the defining condition of any relationship. We live in a hook up and break up culture. Some people pursue an elusive romantic fantasy fuelled by TV and film. Others just want someone to make them feel good about themselves. Let me not point fingers at others and fail to include myself; as a teenager my goal was to find the most beautiful girl I could to be my girlfriend in order to make other guys jealous. Like everything until we find Christ, our ultimate goal is our own ego and maximising our own interest.

But if you're a Christian, your life has been turned upside down by the amazing selfless love expressed by God through His Son, Jesus. Now 'You are not your own' (1 Corinthians 6:19) but you 'belong to Christ' (Galatians 5:24). One of the ways you live for Him is to:

… in humility value others above yourselves, not looking to your own interests but each of you to the interests of the others. (Philippians 2:4)

We must hold on to verses like these when considering going out with someone too.

If our goal is to serve others rather than ourselves, surely 'what kind of boyfriend/girlfriend *should I be*?' is a more urgent question than what to look for in others? Let me challenge you with words you've probably heard many times before, especially if you've been to Christian weddings, from Ephesians chapter 5:

Wives, submit yourselves to your own husbands … (v. 22)

Husbands, love your wives, just as Christ loved the church and gave himself up for her … (v. 25)

God's idea of a romantic relationship is not two people who have found someone to fulfil their needs or make them feel good about themselves – that doesn't come into it! It's instead about two people who serve and submit to one another, honestly and sincerely.

Are you spending your time thinking about your 'ideal guy' or 'ideal girl'? Or are you spending your time working on your own character? Are you learning to be self-sacrificial, submissive and humble? All of us could do with a bit more practice with that, couldn't we?

The more you pursue godliness in your own life, the more you will value and recognise it in others. The Bible says that this quality is true beauty, not the passing attractiveness of physical appearance or superficialities (1 Timothy 2:9–10).

It breaks my heart when I see both guys and girls dressing up immaculately and often, sadly, immodestly in order to win the attention of the opposite sex. In my city this occurs on the streets every night of the week, but I have to confess it happens in my church too. What is the solution? For us to recognise and truly believe that if we are a Christian, then Christ is the most attractive thing about us. So why don't we let Him shine out through our selfless actions and humility rather than attempting to 'catch someone's eye' through our physical appearance?

Of course I am describing the road less travelled but, girls and guys, godliness attracts godliness, so don't concern yourself with outward appearance or a list of other worldy criteria but pursue Him in all things.

2. SHOULD I GO OUT WITH SOMEONE WHO'S NOT A CHRISTIAN?

If you're surprised when I answer 'no' to this question, you've probably missed the whole point of this book. I really want you to pursue living for God in every area of your student life. If you're looking for someone to marry, you're looking for someone who's going to come alongside you in this pursuit so you can help each other along the way. If that's the case, why would you want to get into a relationship and especially a marriage with someone who has no interest in living this way?

For what it's worth, I'll bring out the relevant Bible verses here, but really this one is a no brainer. 2 Corinthians 6:14 exhorts Christians:

Do not be yoked together with unbelievers. For what do righteousness and wickedness have in common? Or what fellowship can light have with darkness?

In farming a yoke is a wooden beam that is put across a pair of oxen in order to pull a load. The two oxen have a single purpose, to plough the field, and this requires two factors to be present. Firstly, the oxen have to be similar. If one ox is big and the other one tiny, then there's an unequal yoking and the partnership won't work. Secondly, they must share a purpose. If one ox wants to walk one way and the other ox a different way, they're going to pull the yoke apart.

Can you see how this relates to relationships and marriage? A successful partnership is dependent on two people who are the same, i.e. are both born again, and have the same purpose, i.e. to worship God. If you're a Christian, an equal yolk is what you're looking for.

I'm not saying that everyone who is not a Christian is not a nice person – by no means! There are lots of great people who are yet to meet Christ. The girl or guy you've met might be the friendliest and nicest in the world.

But when you became a Christian, you became a new creation (2 Corinthians 5:17). You were dead, yet now Jesus has made you alive (Ephesians 2:1–10). A radical change has happened, so don't compromise that or pretend that it's not important. Look for someone who will help you to live for Jesus more, rather than being a hindrance to this call on your life.

3. HOW DO I GET A GIRL TO LIKE ME?

You know what cracks me up sometimes? Christian flirting. Man, that's funny. Funny but tragic at the same time.

More often than not a guy likes a girl but he's either not confident enough in his feelings for her or he doesn't have enough courage to ask the girl out, so he enters into this pitiful charade of 'flirting'. It's often also the case that he wants to protect himself from rejection so he tries to figure out whether she likes him by suggestion, flattery and attempts at humour.

1 Timothy 5:1–2 encourages guys to:

Treat … younger women as sisters, with absolute purity.

This speaks right into the situation of how student guys should behave with student girls. It seems to me that so often girls are led on by guys who are trying to 'pick up signals' and flirt, and consequently go beyond the boundaries of friendships. It then all descends into gossip, misunderstanding and hurt feelings. Guys, honour the girls, don't lead them on! Either a girl is your wife or she's your sister in Christ. We should be able to be honest with one another.

Ask yourself these questions in regards to your female friends: am I treating her with purity? Am I giving her a signal that is not in line with how I feel? If I have feelings for her that go beyond friendship, am I being honest with her? It can be tempting to indulge in the attention of a girl if she fancies you, but playing along with it when you know you don't have the same feelings is dishonest.

Flirting is a concept that relies on temptation, suggestion, hinting and even giving inappropriate physical attention, and it cuts right against verses like 1 Timothy 5:1–2. Flirting's got nothing to do with purity and it's got nothing to do with friendship.

Now there's nothing wrong with being polite, funny, servant-hearted or even charming. But you can do these things as a friend to another friend and leave out any suggestion of romance. Or you can do these with the stated intention of pursuing a friendship and romantic relationship with a girl, but to honour the girl your actions must be in line with your words. Too often a guy is too scared to say something so he suggests it with his actions and a girl gets mixed messages about his intentions. Leaving girls confused about your intentions is not treating her as a sister 'with absolute purity'.

4. SHOULD THE GUY ALWAYS TAKE THE LEAD?

A lot of these questions, and this book for a matter of fact, I've addressed from a guy's perspective. Funny that – I am a guy after all! But I wouldn't want you to think that this book is only aimed at guys, so here's an answer that speaks directly to the girls.

Now look, I'm a complimentarian. Big word, huh? It just means that I believe the Bible says that God has given a husband and a wife two different roles in the marriage relationship. It doesn't mean that one is better than the other or more important to God, but that men and women, and especially how they should function in a marriage, are different.

Anyway, I don't want to get into that now because this book's not really about that, but I do know that in churches where there is that kind of theology going on, guys and girls can be a bit confused when it comes to relationships. Should a girl ask a guy out? What does it look like for men to be men and women to be women in relationships?

Firstly, not as a rule but as a suggestion, I put it to the men to do the asking – not because the Bible says they should, but because I think it is a courageous and honouring thing to do. No one likes getting turned down so it takes some guts to ask someone out. But men, I think it does the ladies a favour when you take that risk and, if you're interested, ask her out. It gives her the freedom to say 'no'. Yeah, you might get embarrassed and it's a bit awkward, but be a man and take it. Don't let her have to suffer the embarrassment of that.

Secondly, although 'dating' as I've described it is aimed at marriage, it's not the same thing. Often girls will want the guy to take the initiative in things but sometimes they won't. Generally, though, it's a good thing for the guy to do.

In marriage the Bible says that husbands should love their wives as Christ loves the church. That means sacrificially. So guys, in dating take opportunities to demonstrate that you will be a sacrificial husband. Offer to pay for stuff, walk her home, don't embarrass her and generally try to put her welfare ahead of yours. Does that mean opening a door for her? Yeah, why not?

Now some of you are probably up in arms at this point and saying that we live in the twenty-first century and this stuff is all old fashioned. But without getting into a debate about feminism, let me say this: treat others how you would like to be treated – that's what Jesus said, right? And it applies to both men and women. Is that even-handed enough? Girls, if you want to split the cost of dinner, go for it! Guys, don't be patronising but do try to out-do her in acts of service. I think that's a God-honouring way to do relationships.

5. HOW DO YOU ASK SOMEONE OUT?

At the risk of undoing my poor attempts in the last answer to be even-handed, let me answer this from a guy's perspective. Ladies, please don't turn the page yet, though – it'll be helpful to know what to look for and what type of asking to say yes to.

Ah, the heady thrill of blossoming romance! This is where the rubber hits the road, isn't it? You like the look of a girl. In fact, let's face it, you fancy her. You've got to know her a bit and you just want to get to know her more because she seems amazing. She's a godly girl with a desire to serve God and be obedient to Jesus. She's on your mind a lot of the time and you just can't shake the idea of what it would be like if you were a couple. Yeah? If not, you're probably not in the right place to ask her out.

Now before you ask someone out, understand that you're never 100 per cent sure if it's the right thing to do. If a guy came to me and said, 'I'm absolutely 100 per cent sure it's right to ask her out,' I'd be very concerned. The fact is you're never certain. The 'what if it's not right?' question will always be in the back of your mind. That's normal, don't worry.

But I would recommend speaking about it to

some godly male friends or older guys in your church. Seek their wisdom about whether they think it's a good idea and if you're in a good place to ask.

If they do give you the thumbs up, my one piece of advice is: be intentional but not intense. If you've resolved in your mind that you want to ask a girl out on a date, then walk up to her at an appropriate moment and ask her to her face. Don't text her. Don't email her. Don't Facebook her. Calling her up is not the worst idea, but speaking to her in person is the best plan. Why? It shows that you're serious and it shows that you're not a coward.

I should probably put some Bible verses in this answer, so how about this one: 'be courageous' (1 Corinthians 16:13). You might not think that has much to do with asking a girl out, but the original Greek word used here (*andrizesthe*) literally means 'act like men'! Of course, having courage isn't all that 'being a man' is about, but it does help us here. Think about it: if a guy hasn't the courage to ask a girl out face to face, do you think that girl is going to think this is a man with courage enough to lead and protect her as a godly husband?

'Being a man' is not about macho-ism, athleticism, intellect, giftedness, etc, but is about having courage. This includes being courageous enough to put your pride on the line and risk getting shot down by asking a girl out.

So be intentional by making your intentions clear. Say that you like her and you'd like to get to know her. Girls appreciate honesty. They appreciate you being real. But don't be intense. Give her a clear question and let her decide her answer. If she wants to go away and think about it, that's fine; give her the space she needs. Don't pressurise her and don't get too worked up!

Let's face it: if you're a godly guy and you're looking for a godly girl, asking her out is a compliment. You're saying that you've recognised godly character in her. You would like the opportunity to get to know her better.

It's not a proposal either! You're not saying that you want to marry her, but that you want to pursue a friendship with her with that end in mind. And if she says 'no', it's not a disaster! I've known many guys who have come away from a 'rejection' and, yeah, it's not the best feeling ever, but actually it is good to know that you had the guts to walk up to her and do something courageous.

11

A Ten-Minute Bible Study

The object of this five-step model is to focus on one simple truth from the Bible. When you read the Bible every day, God speaks to you every day. But by focussing on *one* idea, it makes it easy to discern what God *is* saying and makes putting that into practice achievable too.

Before you start, pray for a moment and ask God to speak to you through the Bible.

STEP 1: CHOOSE A PASSAGE

Gradually work through one book in the Bible,

looking at a little bit each day; don't chop and change. If you've not done this before, it's best to start with one of the New Testament letters like Philippians or Colossians.

STEP 2: READ THE PASSAGE AT LEAST TWICE

If you're reading the New Testament, usually reading no more than ten to fifteen verses gives you plenty to think about. With the Old Testament, you might need to read a chapter in order to understand what's going on. Then read the passage again to make sure that you get what's being taught.

STEP 3: FOCUS ON ONE IDEA OR VERSE THAT STANDS OUT AND REWRITE IT IN YOUR OWN WORDS

Often we feel that nothing stands out in a passage until we put pen to paper. It could be really obvious or simple, but just write it down as if you were explaining to someone else what the Bible says.

STEP 4: REFLECT ON WHAT THAT COULD MEAN FOR YOU AND WRITE THAT DOWN

Notice what you've written and ask yourself questions like, 'Why is that important?' and 'What does this tell me about who God is or who I am?' Answer that in a sentence or two.

STEP 5: WRITE DOWN AN APPLICATION

The goal here is not just to be a 'reader of the Word' but a 'do-er'. It's helpful to ask yourself questions to figure out what the specific application for you is today. For example, does this passage tell you something …

You should believe about who God is?
You should praise, thank or trust God for?
You should pray about for yourself or for others?
You should have a new attitude about?
You should make a decision about?
You should do for the sake of Jesus, others or yourself?

The best applications are 'SMART', which means specific, measurable, achievable, relevant and time-bound. So, for example, instead of saying, 'I need to encourage people more,' you could write, 'I will phone up a friend from my small group today just to encourage them.'

When I do this, I find it helpful to have a notebook that I use each day. So now I've got pages and pages of 'verse', 'reflection' and 'application' for each day. This is especially helpful as I can look back and see if I have managed to achieve my application. It also helps me to identify themes in what God is saying to me. Sometimes we don't realise all that God has been saying until we start keeping a record.

The Bible study guide in the final section of this book will also help you get into Scripture day by day.

12

A Ten-Minute Prayer Time

This isn't an original idea – your granddad's granddad probably did it (if he was a Christian) – but it's lasted because it works. It's not complicated either – it's just a helpful way to construct a prayer time.

It's probably not something to do every single day – it might get too repetitive – but following it a few times a week would be good. I'd advise praying *every day* if you can, but just don't always use this model, that's all I'm saying. Oh, and the other good thing about this is that it's really easy to do with someone else, or even in a group with a few people. Try it out! This is what the model is.

STEP 1: PICK A PASSAGE OF SCRIPTURE

You may be reading through a book of the Bible each day anyway, but the good thing about this technique is you can just literally open the book at pretty much any chapter and get going. Read through about a dozen verses a couple of times.

STEP 2: PRAY THROUGH A-C-T-S

In classic Christian style this is an acronym! That means each letter stands for something. Here's how it works.

A IS FOR ADORATION

Find something in your passage that helps you to adore (worship) God. This is most likely an aspect of His character that the passage reveals. 'God I praise you because you're all powerful' is an example. Your passage might not say something specifically about God, but you should find something that leads you to delight in Him. Then simply pray a few sentences (try and make it more than one or two if possible) of worship.

It's also a good idea to not say anything for a few moments and just dwell on the character of

God. This is what it means when the Bible says 'meditate'. It's not spooky spiritual; it just means thinking about who God is. You'll be amazed at how much this can change your perspective on life when you do it regularly.

C IS FOR CONFESSION

OK, it gets a little bit uncomfortable here but it's a necessary part of the Christian life. Confession isn't about feeling sorry for ourselves or having an obsession with sin. True confession and repentance leads us back to Jesus and our need for Him. Ask yourself the question, 'Is there anything in this passage that reminds me I need to say sorry to God?'

Try and be specific when possible. If it's a passage about God's generosity, don't say, 'God, I'm sorry for being stingy.' Make it real: 'God, I'm sorry I've not been giving to the church this month,' or, 'I'm sorry I've not offered to buy anyone a drink this week,' or, 'I'm sorry I ignored my friend's birthday.'

Finally, don't try to make up for your sin either, for example by saying, 'God I'll give twice as much next time.' Repentance isn't about your work; it's about accepting Jesus' work for you. It may well be a good idea to change your giving habits, but now's not the time to be thinking about that.

T IS FOR THANKSGIVING

It's easy to mix this one up with adoration. I often mess the earlier one up and say, 'God, I thank you that you're so full of grace,' and then I get to this one and get stumped! Don't worry, it's not the end of the world (unless you're reading Revelation – sorry, bad joke). Just look at the passage and think, 'What do these verses remind me to be thankful to God for?'

Like before, try and be specific. For example, 'God, thank you for the friends that you've given me who challenge me and keep me humble,' or, 'Thank you for providing me with my job.' Spend some time being grateful to God.

S IS FOR SUPPLICATION

Christian jargon alert! Don't freak out, though – supplication just means asking God for stuff. This is the part where you can make some requests. Often when we pray just off the top of our heads, this is where we start: 'God, please help me with this … please bless this person … etc.' But hopefully after spending a few minutes adoring God, realising your need for Him and thanking Him, you'll be in a better place to pray with faith rather than just going through your shopping list of needs or wants. Go ahead: make some faith-filled specific requests to God!

STEP 3: **YOU'RE DONE**

Yeah, this is not really a step, but let me just add that you might find it helpful to write some stuff down, particularly prayer requests. Praying with faith means that we have at least some sort of expectation that God will answer. I know a lot of people who like to write down what they're praying for and then make a note when God answers them. This will really help build your faith because God answers prayer – often much more than we realise!

13

Help to Live Porn-Free

Pornography is a massive challenge for many Christian students. I don't have to tell you how easy it is to access or how prevalent and accepted it is in uni life (and beyond).

But as I've said previously, not only does it make a mockery of God's teaching and design for sex, it can also have a powerful effect on your life. Many people who are once exposed to pornography become enslaved to it. A casual mistake develops into a regular habit, and this type of habit can be very hard to break.

If it was down to our efforts to resist or break ourselves free from porn, we wouldn't stand a chance. But thankfully Jesus is our freedom. As children of God we needn't be slaves to anything (Romans 8:15).

Changing habitual sin in your life isn't easy and requires a process – a process of exchanging lies that we believe and love that we have for sin with believing the Truth about God and learning to love and desire Him more than anything else. I have listed some amazing books in the further reading section that will help you on this journey. I highly recommend them as tools to see lasting change in your life.

But let me also highlight some first steps you can take now to help you break your habits.

SPEAK TO SOMEONE ABOUT IT

Live as children of light ... and find out what pleases the Lord. Have nothing to do with the fruitless deeds of darkness, but rather expose them. It is shameful even to mention what the disobedient do in secret. But everything exposed by the light becomes visible ...
(Ephesians 5:8–13)

Much of the power that porn often has over Christians is the secret dimension to it. Because nobody else knows, the consequences seem less severe. At the same time the fear of being exposed actually increases the feeling of shame. This discourages Christians even more, can sap any hope they have of changing and leads them into a deeper cycle of repetitive sin and shame.

But God encourages us to confess our sin. We don't exactly understand why but confessing sin can break much of temptation's power. In confessing you're also admitting you need help and can't beat this on your own. This is an important first step to change. It's not a trusted Christian friend or leader who will be the help you need to change; it's Jesus you need. But this friend can help you find and treasure Jesus when you lack the faith and courage to turn to Him on your own.

There's so much more I could say about accountability but let me just say this: being accountable to someone is not confessing your sin and them saying, 'Don't worry, you're forgiven.' The fact that you're forgiven is one part of the Truth that they should be pointing you to. They should also be reminding you of the Truths that you're a son/daughter of God and this sin is so far beneath you, and that God is not just good but better than what you're giving yourself to, as well as so much more about the character of who God is. The goal of accountability is to become much less sin focused and much more God focused.

BE RUTHLESS

Jesus taught a lot about being ruthless with sin – not tolerating it, not managing it but savagely cutting it out of your life (Matthew 18:8–9). Now, I'm not advocating cutting off any part of your anatomy, but practical steps are vitally important.

If it's internet pornography in your bedroom you're trapped in, get your laptop out of your bedroom. Get the internet out of your house if you can. You've got to be ruthless.

They say it takes three things for a crime to take place: a victim, a perpetrator and a location. It's the same with sin. Remove one of them and the 'crime' can't happen. Remove the necessary parts (your laptop, the internet and a private location) and you'll start to cut pornography out of your life.

As I've already said, the major work of change happens in the heart, and certainly lasting change doesn't take place without this. Yet at the same time porn and masturbation can become a physical dependency issue. Breaking the habit physically can be an important step.

It's probably not very spiritual or a recipe for lasting change but, knowing my competitive nature, I used to mark on my calendar when I last looked at porn and tried to go for as many days as possible porn-free. You might think that when I reached the record, I'd immediately give in, but that's not true! By then I had begun to enjoy the taste of a porn-free life and I didn't want to give that up. By any means necessary wage war against your sin.

GET ANTI-PORN SOFTWARE

On a similar note, making it impossible to access porn makes becoming porn-free a whole lot easier – not easy necessarily, but easier.

Filters like K9 (www1.k9webprotection.com) block content. For this type of thing it's important someone else sets it up on your computer so you can't just type in your own password to get round it.

There is also accountability software like x3watch (www.x3watch.com) that instead of just blocking stuff monitors your web usage and then sends a report to your accountability partner. Again, this has the effect of exposing your browsing so that it doesn't remain hidden. www.covenanteyes.com is another option that I've known people to use.

These days many Christians struggle with their smartphone since you can browse the internet wherever you are on these. But many people don't know that one phone call to their mobile network will enable 'child-safe' internet filtering that blocks pornographic websites. As with the other blocking software, getting someone else to set your password is a must.

REPENT AND BELIEVE

So often we can feel bad about our 'struggles' rather than repenting of our sin. Repenting is turning to Jesus, saying sorry for our sin, embracing His forgiveness and rejoicing in His goodness. Do you do that? Or, after you've given in to temptation, do you just make empty promises to yourself and God that you won't do it again? That's not repenting. That's trying to get rid of your sin yourself – something you can't do.

There is so much to say about this subject, but there is not room here. That's why I'd thoroughly recommend books like Tim Chester's *You Can Change* to really understand how Jesus brings about transformation in our lives. He's even written a book about porn called *Captured by a Better Vision*, which I'm sure is equally as good. There's also a great free ebook looking at porn and masturbation from a Christian's perspective by Mark Driscoll, titled *Porn Again Christian,* which you find at http://theresurgence.com/books/porn_again_christian

Keep turning to God. Keep focussing your life on Him. Keep believing His promises. Keep fighting to love God more and desire Him. We only love sin because our love for God wanes. The more we desire God, the less we'll love sin and even start to see sin the way God sees it, which gives us a godly distaste for it that helps us change.

This is the road less travelled, this is not easy, but it is worth it. It is so worth it. There's nothing extra special about your struggle that means God can't free you from it. But the majority of the time He doesn't change us overnight. He takes the better, more thorough route of turning our affections away from sin and towards Himself. He's doing that in you and He's absolutely committed to finishing what He started.

14

Further Reading

There are so many quality Christian books out there that it almost seems stupid to make a list of recommended reading for you. Speak to your pastor, student leader, family and friends for good ones; life's too short to read bad ones.

So instead of making a really long list, here are just a few books that have shaped my life in a profound way and which I highly recommend to you.

You Can Change by Tim Chester

Although the works of people like Paul David Tripp, Timothy S. Lane and David Powlison as well as books like *Redemption* by Mike Wilkerson are all to be highly recommended, I pick Tim Chester's book because it just makes things so simple.

Change isn't easy, even for Christians, but this book clearly explains why it sometimes doesn't happen the way we expect and what we can do about it. Most importantly of all, it brings us back to Jesus again and again and helps us see that change is His work in us. It's so accessible; anyone can read it and it will change your life.

Fresh Wind, Fresh Fire by Jim Cymbala

There are a lot of great books on prayer, but this book had a particular influence on me when I first read it some years ago. I'm a rubbish pray-er, so I need to constantly remind myself of its importance. This book does just that as it tells the true story of an ordinary guy who found himself in way over his head and turning to God in prayerful desperation. It's so inspiring to read about what God can do when a small church community completely give themselves to prayer. If I'm honest the book does tail off a little towards the end and gets a bit 'preachy', but I guarantee it'll add some fresh fire to your prayer life.

The Cross of Christ by John Stott

Though I know many people who have read Stott's classic, I don't think I've met anyone who's finished it in less than six months. It's quite a lengthy book, but the reason it takes so long is that there's a week's worth of truth to meditate on in every page.

Sometimes we can make the Gospel sound so simple, and amazingly what Jesus has done on the cross *is* simple enough for a child to understand. But at the same time it has so much depth that a lifetime of study won't exhaust its immensity. Stott expertly helps you to plunge the cross's meaning and significance in a way few others could. The author is a giant of a Bible teacher whose love for Jesus and wonder at the cross is evident in every line. This book is essential reading for every Christian.

The Spirit of the Disciplines by Dallas Willard

I'd been a Christian for years and years, then I read this book and it made me take a fresh look at the whole Christian life. It's so good to find a new perspective on things sometimes, and this book helped me to understand the place and value of spiritual disciplines. They're not chores we have to do to keep God happy; they're pathways to deeper and richer Christian experience. Dallas Willard blew my mind.

Becoming a Contagious Christian
by Bill Hybels

As the title rather cheesily suggests, this is a book about evangelism. In fact, it's the best book about evangelism I've ever read. It takes the pressure and hype out of sharing your faith and helps you see that it's a natural thing that every Christian can do. Uni is a fantastic place to share your faith, and this book will help you make the most out of that opportunity.

Part Three:
The Gospel of John in Twenty-One Days

To use these Bible reading notes, read the verses outlined at the start, then take time to work through the commentary. You may also like to read through the rest of that chapter of John.

DAY 1: THE CENTRE OF IT ALL
BIBLE READING John 1:1–5, 14

In the beginning was the Word, and the Word was with God, and the Word was God. (John 1:1)

Where does everything begin? There was a day when you arrived into the world, before which you had no experiences. There was a time when humankind started to dominate the earth and build the many human cultures we see. There was a time which scientists refer to as the 'singularity', from which all matter and time originates. But John's gospel places the beginning here with Jesus the Word. The original word used here, *logos*, means 'the reason why'. John is telling us that Jesus is not only a teacher, a leader or even a saviour but He is the reason, the source (see v. 3) and the meaning of everything.

ACTION
The theme of the Old Testament book of Proverbs is wisdom. Proverbs 8 pictures wisdom as a person and in 1 Corinthians 1:30 we find out that this person is Jesus. As Proverbs has 31 chapters, it fits nicely into most months – why not read a chapter a day and get that wisdom into your life?

DAY 2: MIRACLES
BIBLE READING John 2:1–11

What Jesus did here in Cana of Galilee was the first of the signs through which he revealed his glory; and his disciples believed in him. (John 2:11)

A first-century wedding in Israel would have meant days of celebration. The wine running out would have been an embarrassing failure! Jesus is present at this family occasion when the worst happens. His mum has watched Jesus grow, knowing all the time that He is God's promised king (the Messiah). Could this be the moment for Him to show His true colours? Her suggestion to Him receives a sharp reply – He is in control and won't be pressured. Nevertheless, Jesus chooses to perform His first miracle here, at a party, showing what kind of God He is. John's gospel constantly refers to the miracles of Jesus as 'signs' (see v. 11) because – amazing as they are – they point to a far bigger reality: Jesus is the Creator God Himself.

ACTION
As a Christian you follow a God who came right into the midst of human life. In the gospels we see Jesus present at numerous meals and social occasions, bringing the life and joy of God. What opportunities do you have coming up to do the same?

SIDELINE
Does the possibility of miracles seem far-fetched to you? Consider this argument: if the existence of the Creator-God of the Bible is possible, then surely miracles – meaning the suspension of the laws present in creation – are possible too. Now since to disprove the possibility of God existing means proving the impossibility of that fact, no one can ever rule out the possibility of miracles taking place as well.

DAY 3: GOD'S GIFT
BIBLE READING John 3:1–17

For God so loved the world that he gave his one and only Son, that whoever believes in him shall not perish but have eternal life. (John 3:16)

Motives are an important thing. They give us a window on someone's mind, helping us to see how that person will act in the future. What motivated God the Father to send Jesus, His supremely valuable Son, into a hostile world? The reason is given here: His *love* for His creation, specifically humankind. This is incredible! We are pretty used to thinking of ourselves as lovable, but John tells us in this very book that people firstly did not recognise Jesus when He came (1:10), and secondly actually hated him (7:7). God does not mess around with mere words – He shows His love for us in action. As Paul puts it in Romans 5:8, 'God demonstrates his own love for us in this: while we were still sinners, Christ died for us.' If we have a God who loved us 'back to life' when we hated Him, then we can be sure that He will constantly do good to us for eternity as He has made us His children!

ACTION

Selfless love is a rare and beautiful thing. Can you think of some practical ways to show those around you that kind of selfless love which God has shown to you?

C.T. Studd was a nineteenth-century missionary (and, co-incidentally, an England national cricketer!). Considering the implications for his own life of God's sacrifice, he said, 'If Jesus Christ be God and died for me, then no sacrifice can be too great for me to make for Him.'

DAY 4: WE HEARD FOR OURSELVES

BIBLE READING John 4:7–19, 39–42

They said to the woman, 'We no longer believe just because of what you said; now we have heard for ourselves, and we know that this man really is the Saviour of the world.' (John 4:42)

God's message of salvation as a gift is remarkable in the way that it translates to different people at different times. In John 4 we are given an insight into how Jesus comes into someone's life. He meets the woman at the well and talks to her casually about her life. Soon the questions take on a spiritual and supernatural dimension as Jesus shows her His personal knowledge of her life and His unique ability to bring healing, restoration and fulfilment to her. It is true that God is building a people for Himself, but we enter one by one. The circumstances of your life might be very different to hers but the pull of God is the same: He identifies with you personally, assures you of His unique power to change your life and calls for your personal response.

ACTION
Think about your own story of meeting Jesus. How would you share it with someone interested to hear? How would your sharing be influenced by factors like the available time and the person's level of interest? How might you need to vary the language you used?

SIDELINE
James O. Fraser was a twentieth-century missionary to the Lisu people of south-western China. After early success in sharing the Gospel with these people, Fraser faced years of doubt and difficulty before seeing a revival, the effects of which are still felt. He said, 'Faith is like muscle, which grows stronger and stronger with use, rather than rubber, which weakens when it is stretched.'

DAY 5: HEALING

BIBLE READING John 5:1–9

At once the man was cured; he picked up his mat and walked. The day on which this took place was a Sabbath ... (John 5:9)

Jesus makes it crystal clear that His programme of restoration will not be held back by petty people! He heals a man on the Sabbath day when it is forbidden to do any kind of work – and receives heat for it. In Mark 2:27 He makes the point that God gave the Sabbath to man to serve them and not the other way round. It is a notable feature of His teaching that He constantly unpicks understandings of God's Word that have caused people to expect less of God or to fit Him into their own agendas. In this passage He points to Himself as God, equal with His Father and equally intent on working to bring about the goodness of the Kingdom (vv. 17–18).

ACTION

The work of 'Kingdom bringing' is a spiritual activity. Jesus told His followers that He only did what He saw the Father doing (John 5:19) and the

Holy Spirit is given to believers that they might live in the same way. You know, you can pray now, 'God, what are you doing and how can I join in?' and partner with God. Amazing!

SIDELINE
The God of the Bible is shown to be sovereign over all that He has created. He has the right and the power to intervene in the affairs of humankind and hears the prayers of His people. A.W. Tozer, who was a minister from Chicago, said 'Because we are the handiwork of God, it follows that all our problems and their solutions are theological.' If we want to take God at His word, we should pray for all physical needs, including healing.

DAY 6: TIME OUT
BIBLE READING John 6:10–15

Jesus, knowing that they intended to come and make him king by force, withdrew again to a mountain by himself. (John 6:15)

In the UK we are pretty holiday obsessed – it probably has more than a little to do with the climate. Anyway, the urge to 'get away from it all' – to be restored, relaxed and recharged – is quite universal. In spite of that it is fairly easy to have a holiday which, while not qualifying for an episode of *Holidays from Hell*, ends up being about as stressful as being at work. Add to that the post-holiday blues and you might wonder why we bother going away at all! Looking at the perfect life of Jesus, we see that same need for refreshing that we recognise in ourselves. The difference is that His natural recourse is to seek time in His Father's reassuring, guiding, fatherly presence.

ACTION
Take a look at Psalm 23 in the Old Testament. It is a very famous part of the Bible that in six short lines describes the relationship of every Christian with God. Why not try memorising this short psalm to help keep you on the right track?

SIDELINE
Bill Hybels must be one of the busiest men in Christian ministry. He leads one of the largest churches in the USA, runs huge conferences and has authored many books. How on earth does he find time to be with God? He says, 'A key ingredient in authentic Christianity is time.

Not leftover time, not throwaway time, but quality time. Time for contemplation, meditation and reflection. Unhurried, uninterrupted time.' Perhaps that is how he does so much!

DAY 7: GOD'S WORDS
BIBLE READING John 7:14–18

Jesus answered, 'My teaching is not my own. It comes from the one who sent me.' (John 7:16)

Communication is the lifeblood of any relationship. If the flow of words between two friends dries up, misunderstanding and distance will surely follow. God knows this and – being a triune community Himself – ensures that He is constantly speaking to His people through His Word. The Bible is actually God's truthful revelation of who He is in all His infinity, accommodated to our finite minds. It is amazing that He has communicated with us through accounts of His dealings with people over the course of many years – using their life and times to write His story. The Bible is unlike any other book or collection. Through it the eternal God speaks to us in the here and now.

ACTION
Do you currently meet with any other Christians to discuss the Scriptures? God has given us the Holy Spirit as our interpreter (John 16:13) and when followers of Jesus consistently study the Bible together, a powerful spiritual event is taking place.

SIDELINE
Augustine, who lived in the fourth to fifth centuries AD, wrote, 'Such is the depth of the Christian Scriptures, that even if I were attempting to study them and nothing else from early boyhood to decrepit old age, with the utmost leisure, the most unwearied zeal, and talents greater than I have, I would be still daily making progress in discovering their treasures.'

Day 8: The light of life
BIBLE READING John 8:12–20

When Jesus spoke again to the people, he said, 'I am the light of the world. Whoever follows me will never walk in darkness, but will have the light of life.' (John 8:12)

There are many things that people follow as the 'guiding light' in their lives. For some it is a celebrity who models a lifestyle or set of values they wish to emulate. For others it is an ideology or belief system which seems to get to the truth of how life should be lived. Jesus, unlike the heads of any of the other major religions, points directly to Himself as the only true 'guiding light'. He underlines this exclusive claim in John 14:6, where He says, 'I am the way and the truth and the life. No one comes to the Father except through me.' The promise given here in 8:12 to those who *follow* Jesus is that there will always be a light in front of them showing the right path. His leadership in your life removes fear of what is ahead and replaces it with eternal hope.

ACTION

Take a moment to consider the various 'lights' you live your life by at present. What are you trusting in intellectually? What hopes for the future are driving you onwards? Is Jesus sovereign over these in your thinking?

SIDELINE

Dr David K. Winter, Chancellor of Westmont College in California, suddenly lost his eyesight to disease, just prior to his retirement. At a commencement ceremony he told the crowd of students, 'Walk in the sun of this life with Jesus and have confidence when darkness almost overwhelms you. Don't doubt the things God has said to you in the light.'

DAY 9: BLAME

BIBLE READING John 9:1–8

His disciples asked him, 'Rabbi, who sinned, this man or his parents, that he was born blind?' (John 9:2)

When Jesus' disciples come across a man who has been born blind, their first question to their master is, 'Who is to blame for this?' In the age that we live, people who generally live without reference to God will nevertheless use disasters or other tragic happenings to ask, 'Where was God?' Modern comments like that and the question of Jesus' disciples which we find in this verse both make the mistake of not seeing God as sovereign over *all* of history; they think He's just sovereign over individual lives and times. Things that He allows to happen in this fallen world might seem very confusing to us, but we do not have His vantage point. Jesus answers His disciples' question by saying neither of the options they offer are true – the man is not being punished for His or anyone else's sin, rather God wants to show His power in healing him through Jesus! As the chapter proceeds, we can see the uproar that this causes as God's plans clash with the assumptions of humans.

ACTION
Living in obedience to Jesus means not judging people and circumstances according to the flesh (see 2 Corinthians 5:16). The alternative is to live with the knowledge that God's superintending plan is being worked out in human affairs. In what ways does knowing that make you reassess the life challenges you are currently facing?

SIDELINE
The biblical book of Job is a dramatic masterpiece which examines the problem of suffering in the life of a faithful man of God. Job suffers the deprivation of all that is good in his life for no reason that he can readily discern. His friends make matters worse by suggesting in various ways that it must be something that he has done, while Job himself insists that it isn't. Even his wife tells him to go ahead and 'curse God and die'! Although Job doesn't see how, he knows that God is working and 1:22 says, 'In all this, Job did not sin by charging God with wrongdoing.'

DAY 10: THE SHEPHERD

BIBLE READING John 10:1–11

I am the good shepherd. The good shepherd lays down his life for the sheep. (John 10:11)

Sheep can be pretty stupid. You only have to drive through an area where they roam freely to discover first-hand how unwilling they are to be moved from the wrong path – even when they are faced with a couple of tons of metal moving in their direction! It might not be very flattering to hear yourself being likened to one of these creatures, but God's people are often depicted as the 'sheep of [God's] pasture' (see Psalms 79:13 and 100:3). Is this an image which is just meant to offend and demean? Of course not! But it does show us some home truths about ourselves and our relationship to God. Firstly, children grow up towards independence but sheep always need their shepherd. We are dependent throughout our whole lives on the Shepherd for guidance. Secondly, left on our own we do not know how to rightly protect ourselves from evil, but Jesus, the Good Shepherd, stands in the way of evil for His sheep's protection.

ACTION

How easily led are you? The balance to find in the Christian life is to be easily led by God while not being too easily swayed by the times that you live in. What in God's Word do you find hard to live in obedience to? Do you trust and obey the Shepherd's command even when you don't understand why it is given?

SIDELINE

A.W. Tozer said, 'The man or woman who is wholly and joyously surrendered to Christ can't make a wrong choice – any choice will be the right one.'

DAY 11: ETERNAL LIFE
BIBLE READING John 11:17–26

Jesus said to her, 'I am the resurrection and the life. The one who believes in me will live, even though they die …' (John 11:25)

We live in a time of multiple promises of 'regeneration' – products, experiences and services are marketed to us every day as being capable of enriching and enhancing our lives. It is easy not to notice that these things are vying for the position of 'saviour' in our lives: whether their promise is to save us from boredom, loneliness, difficulty or whatever else, each advertisement tells us of the power of their particular subject to fundamentally change the way we feel. Few people have been crazy enough to point directly to themselves as the answer to the deepest needs and longings of the human heart – the problem being that your inability to deliver would be shown up pretty quickly. Nevertheless, this is what Jesus does. He demands complete devotion and offers complete salvation.

ACTION

If the words of John 11:25 are true, then you as a Christian carry the most vital message that anyone can hear. Jesus' promise in Acts 1:8 is that His followers will receive the Holy Spirit's power to bring news of Jesus' eternal life to those around them. Who has God given you to share the news of this life with today?

SIDELINE

Total commitment to a cause is powerful. John Wesley, the eighteenth-century Methodist, realised that if the people he was leading offered themselves unreservedly to Jesus, they would be unstoppable: 'If I had three hundred men who feared nothing but God, hated nothing but sin, and determined to know nothing among men but Christ, and Him crucified, I would set the world on fire.'

DAY 12: FAME
BIBLE READING John 12:28–33

And I, when I am lifted up from the earth, will draw all people to myself. (John 12:32)

Fame and notoriety of one kind or another are on many people's wish list. TV talent shows continue to lure the talented and not-so-talented alike with the promise of overnight stardom. And, though it looks very different from person to person, it seems that everyone wants to be *noticed*. Jesus, speaking to the crowds about how He has come to bring God's judgement against Satan, tells them that He is to be 'lifted up'. What does He have in mind? Is He talking about His social profile being raised? Is He talking about His popularity ratings? Actually we find the answer back in John 3:14 where Jesus says, 'Just as Moses lifted up the snake in the wilderness, so the Son of Man must be lifted up.' He is talking about the effect of His own forthcoming public execution and likening it to the way God healed the Israelites from snakebites in the desert (see Numbers 21:8–9). Jesus' death made Him arguably the most famous person who has ever lived. But this is no idle, purposeless fame – what He is telling us in this verse is that His death brings about the vital and lasting healing which every human so desperately needs.

ACTION

Who do you look to as an example or a role model? Perhaps it's a family member or a historical figure. What kind of legacy and example do you want to leave? What could you do today to take a step towards that goal?

SIDELINE

Speaking of the heart motivation behind Jesus' famous self-sacrifice on the cross, John Stott, one of the great leaders of the evangelical movement, said, 'Only one act of pure love, unsullied by any taint of ulterior motive, has ever been performed in the history of the world, namely the self-giving of God in Christ on the cross for undeserving sinners.'

DAY 13: FOOT WASHING
BIBLE READING John 13:12–17

Now that I, your Lord and Teacher,
have washed your feet, you also should

wash one another's feet. (John 13:14)

In an individualistic society such as ours, Jesus' commands about living together as God's people can come as a real shock to the system. At the Last Supper which Jesus shares with His disciples in the upper room, He explicitly commands His followers to 'love each another' (15:12). That is the hallmark by which He wants them to be known: their selfless attitude towards each other. How does He illustrate the point? He washes the feet of His followers. It is hard to state how scandalous this act is: a respected teacher taking on the role of the lowest house servant. But Jesus is not just a good teacher – He is the God-man and He is stooping to wash the feet of sinners! What a standard He sets His followers for leadership and friendship.

ACTION
All Christian leadership is servant-leadership. What are some of the ways that you can help your local church by taking on serving responsibility?

SIDELINE
Thomas à Kempis, who lived during the medieval

period, wrote, 'The more humble a man is in himself, and the more obedient towards God, the wiser will he be in all things, and the more shall his soul be at peace.'

DAY 14: A PLACE FOR YOU
BIBLE READING John 14:1–4

And if I go and prepare a place for you, I will come back and take you to be with me that you also may be where I am. (John 14:3)

Knowing where you 'fit' in life is something which pre-occupies our formative years. What am I supposed to focus on career-wise? Who should I spend my life with? Where should I live? Not knowing these things can be a source of real anxiety. As a Christian, it is no different; we will still navigate the same life decisions as everybody else. But Jesus puts this in a greater context in today's verse: He tells His followers that He has secured their place in eternity. It should come as a great relief to realise firstly that history is really about Jesus – it is His story, and secondly that in His view our lives count and we are vital to His plans. Knowing our eternities are secure should give us a real security and confidence when it comes to facing the everyday choices which we have to make.

ACTION
What are the big decisions which you are facing or will be facing soon? Bring them before God in prayer now, knowing that He cares about every part of your life.

SIDELINE
C.S. Lewis, the great Christian writer, put it like this: 'Aim at Heaven and you will get earth "thrown in": aim at earth and you will get neither.'

DAY 15: IN THE VINE
BIBLE READING John 15:1–11

I am the vine; you are the branches. If you remain in me and I in you, you will bear much fruit; apart from me you can do nothing. (John 15:5)

Great leaders will go out of their way to inspire their troops to feel 'at one' with the cause. In his rousing 'We shall fight them on the beaches' speech of 1940, Winston Churchill constantly included his hearers in the 'we' who were so assured of success against the Nazis. Jesus, when looking to vividly convey to His followers the nature of their relationship to Him, chooses the picture of a vine and its branches. The branches are completely dependent upon the vine for life; they are not merely 'associated' but are actually a *part* of the vine. Hebrews 2:11 takes up this theme of Jesus' identification with His followers: 'Both the one who makes people holy and those who are made holy are of the same family. So Jesus is not ashamed to call them brothers and sisters.' This is the whole modus operandi of God with His people – He does not stand far off but identifies Himself with them in the closest possible terms.

ACTION
John 15:5 tells us that to 'bear much fruit' is completely bound up with our closeness to Jesus. Communication with God is a two-way street and we should expect to receive directions in response to our prayers which lead us into greater fruitfulness. Take some time out today just to speak to the Lord and listen to His replies.

SIDELINE
Corrie ten Boom and her family were Dutch

Christians who helped many Jews escape the Nazi holocaust but were caught and then imprisoned. Corrie wrote, 'Connected with Him in His love I am more than conqueror; without Him, I am nothing. Like some railway tickets in America, I am "Not Good if Detached".'

DAY 16: TROUBLE
BIBLE READING 16:25–33

In this world you will have trouble. But take heart! I have overcome the world. (John 16:33)

Few sayings are more realistic and encouraging at the same time! At no point does Jesus sugarcoat the difficulty which will be faced by all people in this world and His believers in particular. In the previous chapter Jesus has told them, 'If the world hates you, keep in mind that it hated me first' (15:18). Sometimes as a believer in Christ you *will* stick out like a sore thumb for following Him. This world has walked far away from God and those walking back to Him are opposing the traffic. But Jesus' word of encouragement for us could not be more reassuring. He says, '… take heart! I have *overcome* the world.' That very opposition which Jesus' followers face has been ultimately and decisively overcome by their Lord at the cross.

ACTION

Do you know a fellow Christian who is suffering at the moment for living out their Christian life? Perhaps you could send them a Scripture message today to encourage them to keep going.

SIDELINE

Recognising the value that God brings to the believer out of times of suffering, William Secker, an Archbishop of Canterbury in the eighteenth century, observed, 'If Joseph had not been Egypt's prisoner, he would have never been Egypt's governor. The iron chains about his feet ushered in the golden chains about his neck.'

DAY 17: JOB DONE

BIBLE READING John 17:1–9

I have brought you glory on earth by finishing the work you gave me to do. (John 17:4)

What a thing to be able to say to God, 'I have finished the work you gave me to do'! The satisfaction that comes from a job well done is only a dim reflection of what it is to be commissioned by God and *succeed* at the task. Jesus pursued His call perfectly, only doing what

God led Him to do and doing it well. As His followers, knowing that we are joyfully accepted by God because of Jesus, we should be supremely motivated to see Him glorified on the earth. It is by the power of the Holy Spirit that we are able to take on supernatural, superhuman tasks and succeed. God's provision for His people is total and, although His call will be stretching for us, He will ensure that as we single-mindedly trust in Him and call on His power, we will overcome and in the end hear Him say, 'Well done, good and faithful servant!' (Matthew 25:21).

ACTION
All of Jesus' followers are called to prioritise the needs of others known to them. Write a list of your family and friends and their needs. What obvious things could you pray and do today for each of them?

SIDELINE
When somebody accused William Carey (a man known as 'the Father of Modern Missions') of neglecting his business in favour of ministerial work, he responded, 'Neglecting my business? My business is to extend the Kingdom of God. I only cobble shoes to pay the expenses!'

DAY 18: BETRAYAL

BIBLE READING John 18:1–6

So Judas came to the garden, guiding a detachment of soldiers and some officials from the chief priests and the Pharisees. They were carrying lanterns, torches and weapons. (John 18:3)

Few things in life are as crushing as betrayal. Someone who you have trusted, laughed with and shared common goals with can let you down in a profound and personal way. When this happens, it is almost too much to bear and you find yourself confused and hurt. For Jesus it was one of His inner circle, the twelve disciples, who betrayed Him. Judas had been part of Jesus' mission for years, spent all of his time with Him and was entrusted with real responsibility. He had seen miracles and heard teaching from God Himself. Nevertheless, here we see him bringing the authorities against his master.

ACTION

Jesus tells His followers that they should forgive their enemies endlessly (Matthew 18:22). Is there someone who has hurt you? Make the decision to forgive them now and pray to God for them.

SIDELINE
C.S. Lewis said, 'To be a Christian means to forgive the inexcusable because God has forgiven the inexcusable in you.'

DAY 19: WE HAVE A LAW
BIBLE READING John 19:1–9

The Jewish leaders insisted, 'We have a law, and according to that law he must die, because he claimed to be the Son of God.' (John 19:7)

Humans have a funny relationship with rules. On the one hand we can react strongly against them – you see a sign saying 'No Parking', 'Keep off the Grass' or 'No Ball Games' and you immediately think, 'Says Who?!' On the other hand we can subtly fall into thinking that we can somehow justify ourselves with God by our own moral performance – by 'obeying the law'. The Bible is very clear that this is not the way that we make ourselves right with God as His standards are too great and our performance is never good enough.

Paul says to the Galatian church, 'Clearly no one who relies on the law is justified before God, because "the righteous will live by faith"' (3:11). What the Jewish authorities are doing in the verse above is actually levelling the law against the Son of God. It is a terrible thing to do and the irony of it is that Jesus is the only one who can fulfil the Law of God for His people, and in no way blasphemes by calling Himself the Son of God.

ACTION
Consider the parable of the Prodigal Son (Luke 15:11–32) and think about your attitude to rules. Do you tend to be like the older brother or younger brother?

SIDELINE
Martin Luther, a key leader of the Reformation in the sixteenth century, fought to restore the true Gospel. In his day the established church turned Christianity into rules and rituals. He said, 'Dear friends, I have said it clearly enough, and I believe you ought to understand it and not make liberty a law.' What he is saying is Christ brings us freedom because He has obeyed God's perfect Law perfectly, on our behalf.

DAY 20: THE EMPTY TOMB

BIBLE READING John 20:1–10

So she [Mary Magdalene] came running to Simon Peter and the other disciple, the one Jesus loved, and said, 'They have taken the Lord out of the tomb, and we don't know where they have put him!' (John 20:2)

In the late 1920s a man named Albert Ross set out to analyse the sources of information about Jesus' death and resurrection. He was very sceptical, and intended to write a paper called 'Jesus, the Last Phase' in which he would prove conclusively that Christian hope was just wild speculation. However, in the process of his studies a strange thing happened; he gradually became convinced of the truth of the resurrection! Eventually the paper meant to disprove the Gospel became the classic book *Who Moved the Stone?*, which he published under the pen name Frank Morrison. History faces us all with the great problem of the empty tomb of Jesus. How we answer the question of why the tomb was empty is perhaps the most important thing we will ever do.

ACTION

Can you think of people known to you who say they have intellectual difficulties in accepting the Gospel? Pray that God will help them and provoke them to know Him personally.

SIDELINE

Contemporary American philosopher William Lane Craig says, 'Three great facts – the resurrection appearances, the empty tomb, and the origin of the Christian faith – all point unavoidably to one conclusion: the resurrection of Jesus. Today the rational man can hardly be blamed if he believes that on that first Easter morning a divine miracle occurred.'

DAY 21: ALL THE BOOKS IN THE WORLD

BIBLE READING John 21:20–25

Jesus did many other things as well. If every one of them were written down, I suppose that even the whole world would not have room for the books that would be written. (John 21:25)

John makes it clear why he has relayed the things about Jesus he has in his account of the gospel – it is so we might *believe* and have life (John 20:31). But he is also keen to tell us in 21:25 that because of how awesome Jesus was in His time on the earth, he has had to be selective. Even in this small detail we are given a precious insight into the nature of God. He is far too big for our creaturely minds to ever fully comprehend, and yet at the same time He allows and wills us to know Him *truly* in the way most necessary to us. It seems that in his parting words to the readers of his gospel John is keen to point them beyond both his account and their own experience. He is urging us as God's people to go forward and to write the next exciting chapter of Jesus' story with our own lives.

ACTION
Consider which biblical book you will study next – there is much more for you to know and experience of the true God in His living Word, the Bible.

SIDELINE
J. Oswald Sanders, a director of Overseas Missionary Fellowship, said, 'Most men are notable for one conspicuous virtue or grace. Moses for meekness, Job for patience, John for love. But in Jesus you find everything.'